Praise for *Smart Networking* by Liz Lynch

"In *Smart Networking* Liz Lynch takes the mystery out of building and leveraging effective networks. She gives readers a step-by-step guide to using networking to reach their goals and help others reach theirs too."

> Al Kelly, President, American Express Company

"I love this book! Nurturing relationships is one of the most important things we can do for career management, and Liz Lynch helps us understand the why, how, when, and what of networking. Liz's conversation examples, technology suggestions, and case studies will help anyone network smart!"

> Jason Alba, CEO, JibberJobber.com,
> author of *I'm on LinkedIn . . . Now What???*
> and coauthor of *I'm on Facebook . . . Now What???*

"Change is the only constant in life but it's easier when you can surround yourself with people who can relate to you and lift you up. *Smart Networking* shows you how to connect with the right people, information, resources, and inspiration you need to make positive changes in your career or business."

> Ariane de Bonvoisin, Author, Founder and CEO,
> First 30 Days

"The foundation of success in all businesses, from the corner store to the corner office, is knowing how to network. Liz Lynch shows how the right blend of in-person and online networking strategies can help you build the business or career of your dreams."

> Doug Sundheim, Managing Consultant,
> The Trium Group

"As a working professional in the business development side of the media, entertainment, and technology industries, connections and contacts are an important business tool if not the most important. *Smart Networking* is an invaluable way to understand and navigate this exciting, constantly changing environment. While I am considered an early adopter to online networking, nothing beats a face-to-face connection. *Smart Networking* explains beautifully how to blend the two to turbocharge your networking results. Everyone from novice networkers to expert connectors can learn something valuable in this fascinating, well researched book."

> Bill Sobel, Founder/Executive Director, NY:MIEG
> and Chief Connections Officer, SobelMedia

"*Smart Networking* is the type of book you'll read the first time and nod your head repeatedly. But you won't stop there. By the second or third pass, you'll have marked all the pages you know you need to use as guidelines for how to build a better network. Liz Lynch has delivered on her promise. Now, it's your turn."

Chris Brogan, Cofounder, PodCamp
www.chrisbrogan.com

"In her typical engaging style and clear prose, Liz Lynch makes it easy to realize the importance of networking and how to do it without having a panic attack or resisting unnecessarily. As someone who manages industry trade associations, we know that the power of networking and the skills set forth in this book will get results. Liz demystifies the process for you and gets you plugged in. She makes networking enjoyable!"

Louis Zacharilla, Senior Partner, Alan/Anthony, Inc.
and coauthor of *B2B Without the BS*

"A must read for anyone in business today. *Smart Networking* readers will benefit from Liz Lynch's insights and gain a better understanding of the *why* of networking, in particular the use of social networks. You will understand that by having a presence online, you will move with the times and be part of the new way of doing business."

Marion Freijsen, Cofounder, The E.Factor
the only global community for and by entrepreneurs

"*Smart Networking* is what all of us should be doing. When I wrote *Relationship Intelligence*™ my goal was to get people to become more intelligent about their relationships. That's what Liz Lynch has done for you in this book. She's a savvy networker who understands both your feelings and your strategic needs. Follow her advice. You will become more intelligent."

Jim Cathcart, author of *Relationship Selling*
and *Relationship Intelligence*

SMART NETWORKING

Attract a Following
in Person and Online

Liz Lynch

New York   Chicago   San Francisco
Lisbon   London   Madrid   Mexico City
Milan   New Delhi   San Juan   Seoul
Singapore   Sydney   Toronto

The McGraw·Hill Companies

1 2 3 4 5 6 7 8 9 0   FGR/FGR   0 1 5 4 3 2 1 0 9 8

ISBN 978-0-07-160294-5
MHID 0-07-160294-1

McGraw-Hill books are available at special quantity discounts to use as premiums and sales promotions, or for use in corporate training programs. To contact a representative, please visit the Contact Us pages at www.mhprofessional.com.

This book is printed on acid-free paper.

Library of Congress Cataloging-in-Publication Data
Lynch, Liz.
   Smart networking / by Liz Lynch.
      p. cm.
   Includes bibliographical references and index.
   ISBN 0-07-160294-1 (alk. paper)
1. Business networks.   2. Social networks.   I. Title.
   HD69.S8L96 2009
   650.1'3—dc22

                                        2008022978

For my husband Chris, who lets me dream big and whose insight, support, and love help make those dreams come true.

CONTENTS

FOREWORD

Networking has always been a part of my life. My first job out of college was as a radio producer for the *Barry Farber Radio Show*; a job I got through a high school friend who had heard about the opening. Through my work at Farber, I got to know Mike Levine of the public relations firm Planned Television Arts, who called frequently to publicize his clients' books. He ultimately asked me to join him at his firm. I took over at PTA after Mike retired, and now nearly everyone who works here got his or her job through someone I know.

I am also now publisher at Morgan James Publishing in New York—and yes, even that came about because of networking. I met the founder, David Hancock, at an event and now we are partners.

The power of networking for me is not just about the successes I've enjoyed. It's also about finding ways to contribute to the success of others. That's how Liz Lynch and I met.

In 2003, I gave a presentation on publicity at a small business conference in New York City. Liz got my attention by introducing herself after my talk; she had a friendly smile and a confident handshake. I was in the process of writing *Networking Magic* with my coauthor Jill Lublin, and Liz had just published her *102 Secrets to Smarter Networking* tips booklet. We stayed in touch, and later I asked her to present with me at the Learning Annex. Over the years, whenever Liz has asked for my advice, I've never hesitated to help her, and to her credit, she's never hesitated to take action. That's what makes me want to help her even more.

While the basics of effective networking haven't changed since I started doing it, the modes of networking have multiplied. The majority of connections I've made in more than 30 years in public relations have come through face-to-face interaction, yet increasingly more of us are taking our networking online. New Web sites and communication devices make it easier to connect with interesting people all over the world and to stay connected no matter where we are.

Smart Networking is one of the first books I've seen that gives weight to both in-person and online strategies, showing readers how to find the right blend for their personal and professional objectives. What's also intriguing about *Smart Networking* is how it approaches relationship building from the unique mindset of attracting people into your network and keeping them there. How do you become someone who people want to network with and whom they want to help? Liz will show you. She does it herself every day.

If I were building my network from scratch today, I'd want Liz to teach me this holistic process of combining both in-person and online networking that attracts people and opportunities automatically. Even for someone with networking in his DNA, getting 24/7 results without the 24/7 effort is a highly appealing concept. We're busier than ever, and there are many more things to distract us from our work. By absorbing the insightful yet practical ideas in this book, you'll learn to connect as effectively on a one-to-many basis as you do one-to-one. Now *that's* smart networking.

Rick Frishman
Founder, Planned Television Arts
Publisher, Morgan James Publishing
Coauthor of 10 books, including *Where's Your Wow!*
and two national bestsellers, *Guerrilla Publicity*
and *Networking Magic*
www.rickfrishman.com

ACKNOWLEDGMENTS

This book would never have seen the light of day without the direct and indirect help of many people.

I'm indebted to Marcelino Elosua for persuading me to write a book in the first place, to Keith Fox who opened the door for me at McGraw-Hill, and to the links in my networking chain that led me to both of them: Susanna Macaraeg, David Teten, Lynn Pollack, Michael Pollack, and David Nagourney.

Thanks to Lloyd Jassin for his superb legal insights, to Stephanie Staal for her invaluable early guidance, to my editor Lauren Lynch—one of the few Lynches I am not related to—for championing this book, and to the entire McGraw-Hill team for bringing it to life.

To success story contributors, my friends old and new, for sharing real-life lessons we can all learn from: Bret Allan, Laura Allen, Laura Fitton, Mike Germano, Ramon Gil, Leah Jones, Patsi Krakoff, Dan Markovitz, Pam Narvaez, Jack Petrie, Beth Polish, Stan Relihan, Tracey Segarra, Pam Slim, Bill Sobel, Jan Vermeiren, and Denise Wakeman. You're shining examples for us all.

To those who submitted tips, tales, and techniques to illustrate my key points: Michael DeCamillis, Sheilah Etheridge, Travis Greenlee, Scott Ingram, Beth Kanter, Paramjit Mahli, Alexa Michl, Edmée Schalkx, Christine Topalian, and many others I wasn't able to include. Thank you for your incredible generosity.

To my wonderful e-zine subscribers, blog readers, workshop participants, and booklet and audio customers across the globe who convinced me I had something unique to bring to the world of networking; and to the many association leaders, conference organizers, and corporate executives who trusted me with their members, registrants, employees, and guests. Thank you for supporting my message and helping me establish a platform.

To the mentors, teachers, and inspirational guides for my speaking, writing, and info marketing endeavors: Tom Antion, Alexandria Brown, Paulette Ensign, Fabienne Fredrickson, Rick Frishman, Fred Gleeck, Allison Hemming, Alex Mandossian, Robert Middleton, David Neagle, Dan Pink, Rob Schultz, Mari Smith, and Alan Weiss. I've learned from your expertise and been motivated by your success.

To my amazing, multitalented assistant, Lorie Fossa, who, if I could clone and sell to other entrepreneurs, would earn me millions. Thank you for making my life easier with your incredible work ethic and will-do spirit.

To my sounding board and sanity check, Beth Polish. Thank you for being there week in and week out with an empathetic ear and encouraging word, whatever I happened to need. I'm grateful for your wisdom and friendship.

To Chris, who I am so very blessed to have in my life and love with all my heart.

And finally, to the whole Lynch clan of in-laws, outlaws, nieces and nephews; to Catherine, Matthew, and all those perched on the numerous branches of the Formantes-Chavez family tree; to my brother Major Gary Chavez, a natural connector and an inspiration to his big sis; and to my father, Emiliano, and my late mother, Marilyn, who gave me the blueprint for a happy marriage and the foundation to be successful in anything I do. I love you all.

INTRODUCTION

A hero is no braver than an ordinary man,
but he is braver five minutes longer.
—*Ralph Waldo Emerson*

Read This If You Hate to Network

Being a late bloomer to networking, I understand the reluctance you
might feel in getting yourself out there. At the first networking event I
ever attended by myself, I lasted five minutes—including the four minutes it took me to check my coat. To this day, I still feel my chest tighten
whenever I think back to that moment: standing at the edge of the room
at the 21 Club in New York City, watching 200 strangers in business
suits converse with seeming ease, willing myself to step over the threshold to join them, but feeling so scared and overwhelmed that I could
barely breathe. So what did I do? I raced down the stairs, grabbed my
coat, pushed open the front door, and waved frantically for a taxi.

Thankfully, I've come a long way since, building two businesses
almost exclusively through networking. But if the thought of facing a
room full of strangers evokes a similar flight response in you as it once
did in me, realize that it's nothing insurmountable. While everyone in
that environment may seem at ease with the process, guess what? Not
everyone is. The only difference between them and you is that they're
in the room.

Their degree of courageousness, comfort, and confidence may look
dramatically higher than yours, but in reality, the difference is tiny. The
difference is at the margin. The difference comes down to knowledge.

You may not be sure what works and what doesn't, and you're afraid of making mistakes. That's fair. And you may have certain misperceptions about what it takes to network successfully that have been holding you back. Here are some of the questions I had about networking when I started, and the answers I discovered along the way:

- *Do I need an outgoing personality?*   Not at all. I'm an introvert, and I'm surprised every day to learn of successful people who are as well. Marti Olsen Laney lists a number of famous ones in *The Introvert Advantage: How to Thrive in an Extrovert World*. Michael Jordan, Diane Sawyer, Bill Gates, and Steve Martin all made the list. Both introverts and extroverts have their networking strengths and weaknesses. While we introverts may hold back from the crowd a bit, we tend to be good listeners. While extroverts might find it easier to start conversations, they may shine the spotlight too long on themselves. What's important about your personality is not how you come across on the outside, but the kind of person you are on the inside that gets others to react to you in a favorable way.
- *Do I need to manipulate others to get what I want?*   I hope not. I hope you're the kind of person who people help because they want to, not because they're forced to. Most people like to help when they can, but you need to be clear about what you need, make sure it's appropriate to the depth of relationship you have with them, and ask in a way that applies as little pressure as possible. That's not manipulation; it's simple respect.
- *Do I have to network all the time?*   Not with these strategies. The goal of this book is to help you get to the point where you're highly effective at developing productive relationships quickly so that you don't have to go to five networking events a month if you don't want to. Smart networking is about putting a plan in place to automatically attract people into your world who want to network with you and making it easier and faster for you to help others in return.
- *Do I have to be a "schmooze"?*   Actually, it's better just to be yourself. I'm not even sure how many of us came to associate this benign Yiddish word, which means "to chat idly or make small talk," with someone who tries to ingratiate himself or herself to others with insincere flattery and attention in order to get what he or she wants. That's not what networking is about. The difference between true

appreciation (good) and "sucking up" (bad) is authenticity. If you feel you have to fake your way through conversations, then networking will be hard for you. But if you can shift your mindset and develop a genuine curiosity to learn about other people's stories, not only will you see their value in the world, but they'll be better able to see yours.

There may be other reasons you've resisted networking in the past. Whatever they are, I hope this book gives you new ways to think and demystifies the process to help change your mindset, raise your comfort level, and inspire you to achieve your own success.

If it helps, keep in mind that I was in the same boat myself only a few years ago. In my early talks after writing my *102 Secrets to Smarter Networking* tips booklet, I never revealed to anyone my utter failure at that first networking event. I could never tell them about that! I was the expert! How was anyone ever going to learn from me if I didn't show that I had come out of the womb with this knowledge?

ADMITTING FAILURE

BEING "THE EXPERT"

But I eventually learned that being real was more helpful than being perfect. The first time I opened up to an audience about that experience, I got a very positive response. Participants approached me after my talk and wrote me e-mails later to say, "Thank you for sharing that story, I can totally relate to that." And, "You've inspired me because I know I don't have to fit a certain mold to network effectively."

Many seemed to appreciate that I had learned to network from the ground up. It gave them confidence and comfort to learn from me because I could give step-by-step advice from my own experience, alerting them to pitfalls that someone with a more natural-born ability might not recognize or appreciate. It also made them believe that if I could do it, so could they.

How many of your own mind games are keeping you hidden from the world? Ask yourself:

- Are you tired of seeing great opportunities consistently go to others?
- Do you want more for your career, your business, or your life than what you have right now?
- Are you ready to build and leverage your network the right way once and for all?

All that's standing in your way is knowledge. Now open your mind, and let's begin the journey together.

Reluctant Networker Gets Religion without the Raging Rolodex

You hold in your hands a tangible result of the principles I cover in this book. Smart networking is my approach to building and maintaining relationships over the long term. It makes networking easier, generates opportunities automatically, and helps achieve higher goals effortlessly. In all honesty, writing a book for a major publisher hadn't really been a goal I seriously considered, but when a contact in Europe made the suggestion and I decided that it was what I wanted to do next, I had the contract within months. All as a result of two different sets of relationships I had built over time but never knew would someday interconnect to make this opportunity happen.

I don't have the biggest, baddest Rolodex, nor do I have Michael Eisner on speed dial. I've never aspired to either one. No disrespect to Mr. Eisner, of course. I once met Billy Crystal in an elevator in Chicago, a few months after the release of *When Harry Met Sally* (one of my all-time favorite movies), and completely blanked out. I had absolutely nothing clever to say. And I didn't have the wherewithal to ask for his card or give him mine.

I'm a relative newcomer to networking. I'm neither an extrovert nor a compulsive business card collector. But that's precisely why I wanted to write this book, to show you that you don't need those things to be successful with networking. When I left corporate America in 2000 to start my solo consulting business, it became glaringly obvious to me after my experience at the 21 Club that I didn't know how to network. What I had learned in my career up to that point was how to work hard and get along with folks so they enjoyed working with me. I even got a few promotions and new job opportunities out of it along the way. But go to networking events and work a room? Never considered it; never wanted to do it. Once I was on my own, however, I quickly realized that I couldn't focus on doing good work unless I actually *had* work. I knew I needed to get clients.

I also knew that I needed networking leverage. Every solo practitioner struggles with balancing service delivery with marketing and selling activities. When you're doing one, you're not doing the other. I knew that if I were networking 24/7, no one would be around to do the revenue-generating work. Yet if I focused too much on doing the work itself, my project pipeline would go dry. I had to find a way to keep my pipeline flowing with the least amount of manual intervention.

So while I focused on improving my networking skills and strengthening my base of contacts—through a mix of experimentation, learning from others, and lots of reading—I also invested in activities that helped people learn about my business and encouraged them to want to work with me. In other words, I learned to network smart so that I didn't have to network hard.

Dorothy Leeds, author of *The 7 Powers of Questions*, believes that questions can change your life. "Better questions provide better answers, and better answers provide better solutions." When I started networking, I asked a fairly traditional question, "How can I become a more effective networker?" From that came fairly traditional answers that always seemed to involve chasing down connections one way or another, from approaching people at events, to asking for referrals, to following up after an initial contact.

I soon learned that this type of "push" strategy with networking, although necessary to some extent, was too time-consuming for me, and I began to ask a different question: "What could I do to also *pull* people in and make networking easier overall?" That's the path this book uncovers.

Imagine. What if you could draw people into your network who were already predisposed to networking with you? What if they did all the work to track you down for new business opportunities? What if you never had to knock on doors again? What if people chased *you*? Not only would networking be a whole lot easier, but it would also be a whole lot more fun.

Sounds great, but how do you get there?

How to Network Smart So You Don't Have to Network Hard

For several years, I've helped demystify networking for many people who've struggled, and I've also helped many who enjoy networking but are always looking for faster results with less effort. The answer isn't about doing more; it's about doing the right things—about being strategic. Let's work backwards, and as Stephen Covey would say, begin with the end in mind.

At the end of the day, why do we network? We network so that we have the relationships in place to help us whenever we need help. What do we need in order to get there? Two things: the skills to build relationships and the skills to tap into them. Everything we do with networking is in service of those two things and how we can do them effectively and efficiently.

A great deal has been written about the first part, building relationships, and I have a lot to say about that myself. But I want to focus just as much on the second part, tapping into relationships effectively. If you know a lot of people but can't get their help, it's a waste of time to keep increasing your number of contacts. On the other hand, if you're highly skilled at getting members of your network to respond to you when you need them, you don't need a huge Rolodex. When both work in combination, there's virtually nothing you can't accomplish.

But you can't network around the clock, so how do you strike a balance? Here's a sneak peek at the smart networking system.

First, Develop a Winning Mindset

Your interest and desire for sustained growth in your business or career have to be strong enough to break the inertia of keeping yourself to yourself. Having a better understanding of what networking is, what it can help you achieve, and what's important to focus on in building relationships so that you can tap into them later if you need to will make it easier to succeed.

Part I delves into the foundational mindset shifts necessary for any technique to be effective. Your mindset is your guidance system, helping you navigate through different situations that might come up in your networking. It will help you understand why the techniques covered in the rest of this book work so well, and it will allow you to operate more on intuition rather than memorization of a strict set of rules.

Second, Maximize Your One-to-One Interaction Skills

With all that we can do online and over the phone, connecting one-to-one in person these days is expensive and time consuming by comparison. Yet in many cases it's still highly valuable because sometimes the best place to connect with someone who's hard to reach is at an event. Therefore, you want to make sure that every time you have a face-to-face interaction, you have the skills to take full advantage of the opportunity. This means being able to introduce yourself with impact to automatically attract the people you're looking for, knowing how to start relationships off on the right foot, and understanding how to nurture those relationships over the long term.

Part II offers a strong starting point for handling these critical networking activities and includes many step-by-step explanations. With the relationship mindset you've developed, you can easily mold and adapt these suggestions into a structure that fits your specific needs.

Third, Leverage Platforms That Expand Your Reach One-to-Many

You can turbocharge your networking by supplementing or transitioning some of your one-to-one connection strategies with those that get you in front of more people on a one-to-many basis. Build some visibility and build an online presence to get known more broadly and deeply. Your network can grow strands in multiple directions in both the real and virtual worlds to connect with more like-minded people across geographies and time zones and bring more opportunities to your doorstep automatically 24/7.

Part III describes high-impact activities you can integrate into your networking schedule to boost your name recognition and attract more people and more possibilities into your life more easily. The focus of these chapters is to let you know how these personal marketing techniques can help with networking and to give you an overview of how to get started. If you're interested in exploring any of them in detail, I've included a number of recommended resources at www.smartnetworking.com.

Fourth, Choose the Right Mix of Activities for *You*

I'm going to tell you right now that you don't have to use all the connection strategies I describe in this book. You don't. Although each concept is important and has a purpose, you know what your strengths are, and there are certain activities you'll enjoy doing more because they're a better fit for you. You also know what your goals are, what you're trying to achieve. Certain activities you'll have to do whether you enjoy them or not, because they'll get you to your goals faster. I want to help you find the right mix.

Rather than leave you at the end of the book asking yourself, "Now what?" or saying to yourself, "I don't have 36 hours in a day to do all of these things, so I'm not going to do any of them," in Chapter 13 I'm going to help you put together a one-page smart networking plan. You'll clarify your goals, identify where networking can help you, determine how to integrate networking into your business activities and schedule, and recognize where you might need additional assistance.

I want nothing standing in your way of getting out there and achieving your dreams as quickly as possible. I know that networking can help make that happen for you. You just need someone to guide you through the process.

Overall, smart networking is for anyone interested in generating networking leverage and increasing results without increasing time and effort. Whether you love to network and are looking for ways to improve or if you don't enjoy networking at all and want to make your efforts count, you'll learn how to build relationships both one-to-one and one-to-many that can help you attract the people and opportunities that can change your life.

PART I

CONNECTING WITH ONE'S SELF

MASTERING THE INNER GAME OF NETWORKING

LEAVE YOUR RESISTANCE AT THE DOOR

LETTING GO OF BELIEFS THAT SABOTAGE YOUR PROGRESS

> Life begins at the end of your comfort zone.
> —*Neale Donald Walsch*

Do you live to network or network to live?

There's no right or wrong answer. You can be successful either way. But you have to ask the question and be honest with yourself. I'm not worried if you fall into the first group, of course, since getting out there is not a problem. Networking is a lifestyle. It's part of your DNA. I'm actually not so worried about the second group either. You may not get out as much, but if you're able to develop strong relationships that support your goals, that's what matters.

Personally, I network to live. There are other things in life I live to do—eat well, travel, spend time with my husband—but networking isn't one of them. People are surprised when they hear that I'm not always networking. For me, it's a way to reach a goal, not a goal in itself. So there are specific times I set aside for networking events and meetings, and when I'm there, I'm fully immersed. But that time doesn't blend into my personal life, at least not on purpose. Have I learned of opportunities appropriate for me or someone in my network while I was out with friends? Sure, but that's never the objective; being with my friends is.

While you can be successful whether you live to network or network to live, it's difficult to be successful in your career or business if you don't network at all. That's the group I'm most worried about. If you just haven't gotten around to it yet, let me ask you this: when were you going to start? Your plan may be to stay right where you are, but that might not be your employer's plan. Job security is a thing of the past. The only security we can count on now is our own ability to adapt quickly, and those who can't will struggle. Sooner or later you'll either *want* to make a change or *have* to make a change, and when you do, you're going to need the help of other people to get you to that next level.

What's Holding You Back? Skill or Will?

What keeps people from networking effectively, or at all, is sometimes simply a skill issue. For example, when I'm asked for tips on what to say to exit a conversation gracefully or how to be more memorable, I know that the people asking the questions are looking for an edge that will make them more proficient with networking.

It's a different issue, however, when I hear questions like these:

- "I mostly don't have any interest in talking to anyone at a networking event even though I know that's the whole point of attending. How do I get past that?"
- "So I've introduced myself and said 'hi.' Now what? I am truly not interested in anything the person, who may be a valuable networking asset, has to say."
- "How do you break the ice and not seem like a networking machine?"

Believe it or not, these are actual questions asked by real people. When I hear them, I recognize that their aversion to networking overrides any benefit they can see to making new connections. It's a lot like exercise. Some people really love it, but for many, it's something they know they must do for good long-term health. They'll slog to the gym and try to enjoy their workout as best they can.

Networking takes that same kind of motivation and mindset to move forward even if it isn't the most exhilarating thing on your to-do list. Before any technique is going to be effective for you, you need to overcome the mental hurdles and find the will to network. I can teach you how to write the perfect follow-up e-mail, but if you don't want to get out there in the first place, you'll have no one to send it to.

Look, I've been there. In one of my corporate jobs, I had to attend numerous conferences with colleagues to prospect for potential partners for our company. I hated that. Even though the conferences were designed as networking events where people from different parts of the same industry could meet and collaborate, it didn't seem that easy to get people to meet and collaborate with me. I didn't know what to say to get them interested in what I or my company had to offer.

But that's a mindset issue. Back then, I thought that networking was about people getting together to pitch their wares, like a white-collar flea market, so that's how I operated. It wasn't about a relationship; it was about a transaction. No wonder it was so uncomfortable. I could do that job so much better today. I would have asked more questions, listened more carefully, and then followed up later with the contacts whom I could add the most value to based on what they said they needed, not what I wanted to sell them.

The skills are the easy part, and you'll learn some powerful ones in this book. But the will to start? That's something only you can ignite. How do you make the shift? By opening your eyes to what's happening around you.

Resistance Is Futile; Networking Is Here to Stay

As much as you might prefer to leave networking to others because you feel it's just too unsavory for you, consider the dangers of burying your head in the sand. In the old days, our fates were determined at birth and traditions directed our lives. Folks had little control over what they could become. If you were born into a blacksmith's family, you became a blacksmith, unless you were a woman, of course. Then you were married off to another family to do the cooking and cleaning.

Today we're able to forge our own paths, and new rules are being made up every day. Unless you're wealthy enough to opt out altogether or you've reached your pinnacle of success, you're going to need to network. Here are three big reasons why:

1. Higher Creativity + Greater Speed = You Can't Do It All Yourself

Peter Drucker once said that we live in a knowledge age. Increasingly, our jobs have become less rote and require us to be more creative and more resourceful. Combine this with rising global competition, and we all need to deliver more with greater speed and to think on our feet more quickly in order to respond to new challenges. More is expected of us every day.

What this means then is that you can't do it all yourself. Even if we could boost our brain power with more breathable air and less reality TV, we still have only one body. We can't do two things at the same time in two different places. Until we can clone ourselves, getting other people to help us will have to be the next best thing. The greater your ability to rally people to your cause, especially when they do it because they want to and not because they have to, the greater your chances of success.

2. Information Is Currency; Relationships Are the Clearinghouse

The faster the world moves, the more you need relationships to gather information and filter it for you. Timothy Ferriss, author of *The 4-Hour Workweek*, is the ultimate don't-do-it-yourself guy. He recommends that we eliminate what doesn't need to get done and outsource what does so that we can spend more time on the things we enjoy. He's also a proponent of what he calls the "low-information diet" and limits his time checking e-mail and reading magazines and newspapers. One of the ways he gets information when he does need it is by talking to people he trusts. Instead of following 14 months of minutiae in the 2004 presidential elections, for example, "I let other dependable people synthesize hundreds of hours and thousands of pages of media for me," he writes.

The more information you're able to get both when you want it and when you're not even looking for it will be invaluable to your career or business. Information such as who might be hiring, what your clients are doing, and what projects people are working on inside your company will help you make better decisions about what *you* should be doing.

3. More Ways to Communicate Means That It's Easier to Be Left Out of the Conversation

Before the prevalence of the Internet, finding people to get certain jobs done, such as fixing a broken window or printing your corporate stationery, was limited to looking in your local phone directory or asking someone you knew. Now, not only is it easier to find people, but it's also easier to find out what other people think about them. Were they respectful or rude? Reasonable or a rip-off?

Today, people still ask those they know for recommendations, but with so many of us on information overload and, according to marketing guru Jack Trout, exposed to 4,000 marketing messages a day, if you're not top of mind because you haven't been very visible online or in person, your potential recommenders will forget you exist.

Or, say you're trying to market your business and a journalist is looking for an expert in your field for a story she's writing. If you don't have a blog for her to review how you think and determine whether you're the right source, she'll ultimately go with someone who does.

On the job-search front, recruiters have always been focused on finding people for jobs and not jobs for people, a common misconception. They would much rather fill an open position with someone who already has a job rather than with someone who's out of work. Networking sites like LinkedIn are making it easier to find these passive job seekers, and you can't be found if you're not there.

It's hard not to notice that there are more and more ways to network today, with more ways than ever to be found, be known, and be connected. But there are also more and more reasons to network as well, and the people around you are leveraging these trends to move their lives and careers forward. If you have any aspirations for the short or long term and you're not taking steps to line up your support right now, you'll be starting off with one foot in quicksand. Rather than continue putting off the inevitable, why not learn how to make networking work for you once and for all? Get in the game now before you get left behind.

Give Yourself Permission to Try

Most negative perceptions people have about networking come from fear. I once heard Mark Victor Hansen, coauthor of the *Chicken Soup for the Soul* series, define fear as "false evidence appearing real." In doing more research online, I discovered other appropriate acronyms at AcronymFinder.com:

> Failure expected and received
> Finding everything a roadblock
> Finding excuses and reasons
> Face everything and recover

Whatever you may fear about networking—and I've felt it myself—I want to tell you that it's okay. Underneath that fear, however, is a reality that is waiting for you to shine a light on it. You don't have to get over your fears completely; just know that there are great things waiting for you on the other side if you can manage to take that first step.

Fear: I don't want people to think I have an agenda.
Reality: It's okay to have goals. Everyone does.

Some people resist networking because they don't want to be seen as having an agenda. Somehow, this innocent word has gotten a bad rap as in, "He had an *agenda*," or "I didn't want to push my *agenda*." The *American Heritage Dictionary* defines *agenda* as "a list of things to be done." That doesn't sound ominous to me, quite honestly, but if it bothers you, try replacing it with the word *goal*. Now when you say, "He had a *goal*," or "I didn't want to push my *goals*" it sounds really silly, doesn't it? Of course we have goals. Anyone with any ambition to make life or career improvements has goals.

Even though the two words aren't entirely synonymous—*American Heritage* defines *goal* as "the purpose toward which an endeavor is directed; objective"—for the purposes of networking, they're close enough. An agenda just takes a goal further along in execution. You need to compile a list of the things to do to reach a goal anyway so you will know how to move forward.

Although the literal definition of *agenda* is pretty harmless, if *goal* sounds better to you, go with it and strip *agenda* right out of your vocabulary. No need to think about it ever again. Tell people you're pursuing a goal, or less ominous, that you're working on a project. That way, you won't sound so menacing, especially to yourself. It's all just semantics anyway.

Fear: I don't want to appear helpless, or worse, desperate.
Reality: It's okay to ask for help.

Asking for help is not a sign of weakness. None of us can achieve our goals completely on our own. Even world-class athletes need help from coaches, trainers, team members, and their families. On the other hand, none of us can expect our goals to be delivered to us on a silver platter while we lounge in bed all day eating bonbons. We have to take responsibility for moving ourselves forward. If people sense that you have a clear goal and a plan to get there and that you've been taking action and are ready to take more action, they're less likely to see you as helpless or desperate. And they'll be more willing to contribute when you ask for their help.

Fear: I need to feel totally comfortable first.
Reality: You get comfortable only by doing.

Feeling awkward is normal. Before a skill can become second nature to the point that experts call "unconscious competence," you'll often have to stumble through a period of "conscious incompetence." Do you remember the first time you rode a bicycle? Do you remember how hard it was to coordinate your pedaling and your steering to stay balanced? You probably fell off a few times, or crashed into things, but with a little practice, soon you were able to ride around the block.

It's very unlikely that you could have ridden a bike perfectly the first time you tried just by thinking about it. It's not an intellectual activity. It involves mind-body coordination. While networking may be slightly more intellectual, it still takes coordination. You won't ever get comfortable without doing. Throughout the book, I give you details about what "doing" means, so that when I say something like, "Start reconnecting with people you know," you actually have steps to follow to help you do it. But despite my directions and encouragement, accept that you might feel awkward at the start of any skill-building endeavor. Accept that you won't be perfect. Accept that doing is the only remedy to your discomfort and that practice makes progress.

Fear: It will take too much time.
Reality: You don't have to network all the time.

Are you ready for another confession? It probably won't shock you much at this point: I rarely speak to strangers on airplanes. I'm the kind of person who needs downtime to be alone with my thoughts. Once I've settled into my window seat, my first desire is usually to bury my nose in the latest Seth Godin book or brainstorm key actions for my next project, not to talk to my seatmate. Of course I'm never impolite; I just don't encourage conversation.

I know, I shouldn't do this, right? Have I missed the chance at a million-dollar consulting contract because I didn't strike up a conversation with the person sitting next to me? Perhaps. That's a risk I'll take because that's the best way I've found to preserve my energy in order to be fully focused when I'm purposefully networking; and I've done just fine without it.

Some experts say that you shouldn't compartmentalize networking into such distinct situations. They argue that you should always be doing it—networking with everyone around you everywhere you go. That just doesn't work for me. That may work for you, and if it does, that's terrific. Keep doing it. I won't tell you not to. However, I've found it tremendously helpful to compartmentalize. If I didn't, I'd collapse. I'm certainly interested in meeting new people and learning about them, but I'm not up for doing it all the time, not on planes, not at church, and not when I'm out with my husband. I network to live, remember? I don't live to network.

When I do put myself in networking situations, however, like going to an industry event or having a one-on-one meeting, then I'm there 100 percent. That's time I've dedicated to myself and to the people I'm with to learn about them, have them learn about me, and see if there are ways we can help each other. This means that I'll never take a phone call in the middle of the conversation, and I'll always try to ask questions that help me learn about them on every level. What are their goals? What drives them? Where do they need help?

If you want results from networking, you're going to have to get out there. If you need to reserve your strength, energy, or sanity, then be deliberate about when you choose to network and commit to being present 100 percent.

Fear: I might fail.
Reality: You might succeed.

I once sat next to a woman at a book marketing conference who told me that she was close to completing her book but was concerned that it might become "too successful" and that she'd be forced to travel all over the world and give speeches. She didn't see that she could shape her success to look like anything she wanted. She saw it as a force that would act on her and consume her rather than as something she could create from within.

The truth is that you define your own success. If success means having the most famous people in the world within a few keystrokes of your BlackBerry, that's terrific. If it means never having to network again, that's fine too, although you realize that you'll probably have to network to get there, don't you? The only way to really fail at networking is not to do it at all. Even if you do stumble a few times, learn from your mistakes and keep trying something different until you find what works best for you.

On a final note, another fear you might experience is the fear of rejection. You might reach out to someone who doesn't respond or can't help you. None of us likes to feel rebuffed, but as you get more experienced with networking, you'll learn two things. The first is not to take it personally, and the second is the "rule of next," meaning put it behind you and move on. If you follow the concepts in this book, you'll always be able to find another way to get the help you need.

You Can Do This; You've Done It Already

If you think of a network as a support system of people you can turn to for whatever help you need—insight, advice, information, recommendations, and feedback—then networking is simply the process of building and maintaining that support system.

You have a network already. People you've gone to school with, worked with, play tennis with, or live next door to. No one starts from square one. Even I didn't.

When I launched my business, because I had failed so miserably at my first attempt to network with new people, I decided to take a step back and reconnect with those I already knew. I met with about a dozen former classmates, bosses, and coworkers to let them know that I had made this career change and to ask for their advice. Notice that I said "advice." I never asked directly for consulting work (this is a deliberate strategy you'll learn more about in Chapter 8), but wouldn't you know it? Nearly all of the clients I got in my first two years of business came as a result of those first few meetings. People either hired me directly or referred me, even as much as a year later, to others they thought could use my services. That was an eye-opener for me. I never knew I had such a powerful network. And you have one too.

You may be thinking, "She went to Stanford and worked at all these big companies. Of course her network is powerful. I don't have that advantage." Let me tell you something. No one in my network is a household name. You don't need Warren Buffett's Rolodex to be successful in life. Even he didn't have all the contacts he has today when he started out; he worked to build them. Rather than pine for the network that you don't have, appreciate and leverage the one that you do. It's powerful enough, believe me.

The fact that you have some type of support system in place right now means that you already know how to network to some extent. You may not know exactly how you built your network or even how to access it effectively. You probably don't have all the people you need or have a systemized way to add them effortlessly and deliberately. It doesn't matter whether you like networking or not or whether you're an introvert or extrovert. You have the ability inside you right now to network effectively to reach your goals. I'll help you channel your existing abilities and hone them so that networking works for you.

If you've ever had any doubts about what you can accomplish, you can leave them behind right now.

CHAPTER 2

GAIN A NEW PERSPECTIVE

FRESH INSIGHTS THAT CAN CHANGE YOUR POINT OF VIEW

> He who cannot change the very fabric of his thought
> will never be able to change reality.
>
> —*Anwar Sadat*

What do you want? Whatever it is, chances are that networking can help you get it.

Mike Germano got elected to public office at age 23. Paramjit Mahli got her green card with help from a trustworthy immigration attorney referred to her by someone she met at a seminar. Scott Ingram of NetworkinAustin.com found his wife—his greatest networking success to date. "She was literally referred to me," he says. "Sometimes the results of your networking efforts go beyond your wildest expectations."

Perhaps you want help for someone else—a child, a spouse, a friend. Your network can help others too. Beth Kanter, a nonprofit consultant; Chris Brogan, a social media expert; and 81 others raised enough money in 24 hours through online networking to send two Cambodian kids to college. The beauty of relationships is that help can come *through* us, not just *to* us, and we can be a conduit for someone else's success.

Help Can Come in Many Forms

We know the obvious ways that networking can help: to get more customers for our business or find a new job when we need one. But few of us realize the full power that our networks have to change our lives and the lives of those we care about.

Relationships Provide Us with *Support*

From the examples I mentioned, you can see the range of support our networks can give us with any goal we set for ourselves. Whenever I speak to entrepreneur groups, I remind them that although we can start a business alone, we can't grow a business alone. We need support in the form of people—vendors, suppliers, subcontractors, employees, and perhaps investors—and in the form of information—advice, ideas, and feedback.

Support from your network can help you make better decisions about your business. Relationships can also help in weighing alternatives and avoiding pitfalls with career decisions, especially when you can turn to someone who's already gone through the experience or has a unique point of view.

Relationships Help Us with *Influence*

We might not have access to the decision maker, but having a relationship with someone who knows the decision maker and can put in a good word for us can often be more beneficial. That person's recommendation will be more like a third-party endorsement—someone else saying that you're great, which is more believable than saying so yourself.

During my senior year of college, I interviewed for a five-week internship at the accounting and consulting firm Arthur Andersen to take place during our winter break. Even though I wasn't a business or accounting major, I had taken a few accounting classes as electives toward my engineering degree. I had always intended to go into the business world after college and thought that having some big-firm business experience on my résumé would help. My roommate's boyfriend had joined Arthur Andersen a year earlier and made a call to the manager who had interviewed me. I was one of only two people from UC Berkeley to get an internship, and I credit Mark, now my former roommate's husband, with helping me. I strongly believe that that brief internship helped me land a job at Goldman Sachs after college, which helped me get into business school, and so on. It's amazing how one phone call can influence the rest of one's life.

Relationships Provide Us with *Resources*

You can find almost anyone you're looking for through your network. And today, online networking sites like Facebook and LinkedIn make more of the world available to us, allowing us to find resources not just for ourselves, but for those in our network as well.

NETWORKING SUCCESS STORY |
CONNECTING THROUGH POWERFUL PLATFORMS
Stan Relihan, President and CEO
Expert Executive Search
Sydney, Australia

Last year Stan Relihan was interviewed on Cameron Reilly's *G'Day World* show on The Podcast Network, on the subject of using LinkedIn as a business tool. During the interview, Cameron, a real LinkedIn skeptic, presented him with a challenge: use the LinkedIn network to find the most impressive celebrity guest to appear on Cameron's show, which covers science, technology, politics, religion, and the media.

"This was a real test of the quality and depth of the LinkedIn network, as well as the willingness of the LinkedIn community to help with introductions," says Stan. Through his LinkedIn connections, Christian Mayaud at The Verticom Group and Cynthia de Lorenzi of Success in the City, Stan was able to connect with Vint Cerf, widely known as the "father of the Internet" and chief Internet evangelist at Google, who appeared as a guest on Cameron's show a month later.

As a result, Stan now has his own weekly podcast show on business networking and Web 2.0, called *Connnections* which is currently third on the list of Digg.com's most popular business podcasts, ahead of *BusinessWeek* and *Wired* magazine. He owes this all to LinkedIn.

When you help people get things done, you develop a reputation as a go-to person, someone with access to the right resources. You enhance your credibility and create opportunities for those around you, and like Stan, you can receive unexpected benefits for yourself in the process.

Relationships Help Us Get *Information*

If you have a question that needs a quick answer, do you have access to an expert you can call on the spot? Whether you're looking for insights on the latest industry trends for a new product launch or firsthand accounts on working with a new business partner or potential job candidate, your network can help you get the information you need to make better decisions.

Members of your network can also help you get information you didn't know you needed. Did you ever get the inside scoop on an upcoming opportunity that few people knew about? A few summers ago, my husband and I were having dinner with another couple from business school, Lynn and Michael. As we sipped wine on their deck and got caught up on each other's work, I told them about some of the consulting projects I had worked on in the last six months. As I talked, Lynn turned to Michael and said, "Maybe she'd be able to help David," a friend of theirs who had recently landed a senior position at a media company. "He's working on their new strategy and was looking for some help," Michael said, "I'll give him a call and see if he still needs people." That assignment turned into my biggest project to date, and I didn't even know that opportunity was out there until my friends gave me the heads up.

As good as we are, as brilliant as we are, we can't do everything ourselves. Relationships can help us with so much we want to accomplish in life and business if we know how to draw on them.

Relationships Built to Last

Are you able to get your network behind you for whatever it is you want to do? In my experience, I've found that you don't need a huge network if you have a responsive one. In fact, in *The Tipping Point*, Malcolm Gladwell talks about the "rule of 150" as the maximum number of people with whom one can have "the kind of relationship that goes with knowing who they are and how they relate to us."

Just about everything you need to be successful with networking boils down to one question: What kind of person would you need to be for someone to be willing to help you more than once?

Even if you never ask for anything, this question is a great way to orient yourself toward building relationships in general. Why? Because by focusing on the first "ask," you end up thinking only about yourself. You think about the transaction, about getting something done for your benefit at any cost. But if you force yourself to think beyond that, to the requests you might have to make later, you'll think more about the relationship. How would you have to treat that person in order to be in a position to ask for something else down the road?

In other words, how would you build relationships that last? For starters, you'd be sure to treat people with respect and appreciation. You would give them your attention and make an effort to learn about them. You'd never make uncomfortable requests, never take up too much of their time, and always be generous in your interactions, saying *please, thank you,* and *great job* when appropriate.

And when the time comes, you'd be helpful and responsive to their requests. If they asked you for help, you would be prepared to do whatever you could to assist. From a practical standpoint, they may never ask you for anything, but it's all about your willingness to be "on call" that matters.

Being successful with networking is not about being flashy or charismatic; in fact, it's not about you at all. It's about how you make others feel when they're around you.

When I worked at *Money* magazine in the late 1990s, our publisher at the time, Geoff Dodge, asked me to speak a number of times to students from his alma mater, Babson College, who would take field trips from Boston to New York City to learn about the inner workings of a magazine. Although I was terrified of public speaking, I was happy to help mold young business minds and, of course, help my boss's boss where I could. A few years later when I started my consulting business, Geoff was one of the first people I called for advice and the first one to hire me. By then he had left the magazine to run an entrepreneurial company in the advertising industry. He also directly and indirectly helped me get two more engagements after that. Five years later, we ended up working together again. That's emblematic not only of Geoff's generous nature, but also of the kind of long-term relationships we both strive to build.

In stark contrast to this, Christine, a former colleague, dealt with someone in her network who was clearly in it for the short term. She saw a job on LinkedIn that she felt she was perfect for and contacted a freelance recruiter in her network for help. He was also part of the hiring manager's network, but different from the in-house recruiter listed for the position. Her recruiter was thrilled with her background and told her that she would definitely get an interview. Weeks turned into months with no interview in sight. Christine didn't know that her application was in limbo because the recruiter wanted to present her as his candidate in order to get a referral fee. But the company didn't want to use an outside recruiter, which is why it had posted the position on LinkedIn in the first place, to get candidates directly.

In effect, without telling her, the recruiter was willing to let Christine lose out on the job if he couldn't get a fee. He sacrificed a long-term relationship for a potential short-term gain at her expense. Once she found out, two months into the process, she acted quickly on her own to rescue her candidacy and get the job without him. By not taking the long view, the recruiter permanently damaged his relationship with Christine. Should she or anyone she knows need an outside recruiter to fill a position, he certainly won't be on the list.

Think Give *and* Receive, Rather Than Give *to* Receive

There's generally a great deal of emphasis placed on the "giving" part of networking in most books and articles, and admittedly, there's a healthy dose of it in this one as well. I'm a firm believer in giving. It feels great to give. But I'm just as big a fan of receiving. I think there has to be a balance, or you won't participate.

For some who are new to networking, the oft-repeated notion of, "Give first, receive later," can be a huge obstacle in getting started because they don't fully understand it. They take it too literally. Let's say, for example, that Carol is a newly minted college grad attending a conference. She's always wanted to meet Amy, a prominent expert in Carol's field of study who's also attending the conference, to get some career advice. Carol is new to networking, but she's heard over and over that you have to give to get. She has yet to approach Amy, however, because she hasn't yet figured out what she can give her. "What could Amy possibly want from me?" she wonders. And she never makes her move.

What would we do in her situation? Simple: leverage a new insight. Instead of getting all tangled up in give *to* receive, adopt a whole new way of thinking called give *and* receive, which can be viewed in two ways.

First, think of giving and receiving as two sides of the same coin. What one person gives, the other receives in turn. At the start of a relationship, Carol can offer Amy the simplest gift: appreciation. Anything more is presumptuous anyway. In *How to Win Friends and Influence People*, Dale Carnegie noted that one of the deepest desires human beings crave is a feeling of importance. When we seek advice, as Carol wants to do here, we are feeding that need. In the process, we start a dialogue that enables others to share their knowledge and gives us a chance to learn more about them. Only then can we identify what value we can most appropriately offer.

Second, think about giving and receiving not person by person, but within a whole system. Someone may offer you help before you have a chance to help her or him. By the same token, you may give help to someone and never ask for anything in return. This should all be okay. You're never going to have an equal balance of giving and receiving with every person in your network. It's unrealistic to expect that, and you shouldn't be keeping score anyway.

Networking isn't purely altruistic, but it's not charity work either. We do expect to get some return from our efforts, or we wouldn't be doing it. What we should strive for is a networking ecosystem that's in balance, that involves giving *and* receiving, where help flows within our network wherever it's needed. If we need it we ask for it (appropriately, of course, which we'll discuss in Chapter 8), and if others need it, we offer it. That should be the natural outcome of building relationships that last.

The Pull of Networking Gravity

At the end of the day, we're all counting on our networks to come through for us when we need them. Therefore, it's smart to keep working on strengthening our position by making new connections and cultivating existing ones. But all of our work is for naught if we can't get the right people into our network in the first place and keep them there, or if we can't get the help we need when we need it.

When I first started my business, I was frustrated by how much time networking took. Going to early morning breakfast meetings every week, following up with referrals who weren't a good fit, and having to explain my business over and over again to people one by one. I thought there had to be a better way to use my time and get a bigger bang from my efforts. How could I network smart so that I didn't have to network hard?

I took a step back from those tactics and began to look at networking more strategically. I asked myself the same question my management consulting clients ask me about how to maximize business opportunities: "Since we can't focus on everything at once, what's the best way to deploy our limited resources of time, people, and money to reach our goals?"

When I looked at networking through this lens, the answer was obvious: by attracting people into your world who are already predisposed to networking with you based on the value you can bring to their life and the value they can add to yours. It goes back to the foundation of networking that relationships should be mutually beneficial.

When people contact me because they've heard me speak, read my blog, or were referred by a friend, they already have some idea of how I can help them and/or how they can help me, so we're well on our way to building that mutually beneficial relationship. If we're meeting randomly on the street or at an event, on the other hand, we have to start from square one. Not that there isn't value in this, but it just takes longer, and there's a limit to how much you can network no matter how good your skills are. There are only so many hours in a day.

Rather than focus on just building your network, focus on building your networking gravity at the same time. *Networking gravity* is a force that draws people automatically into your world with whom you have the greatest potential to build mutually beneficial relationships. You build that gravity by:

1. Sharing your expertise widely so that people understand what you do, whether it makes sense to initiate a connection with you, and how you might be able to help each other.
2. Having a clear idea of the kinds of people you want to meet and showing up in places where they can find you and you can find them.

3. Developing strong interpersonal skills that allow you to turn initial meetings into lasting connections.
4. Raising your profile to attract people in large numbers and enable you to stay top of mind.

Last fall I received an e-mail from the programming chair of the Massachusetts chapter of a national professional organization. She had found my blog, made it to my Web site, and contacted me by e-mail about facilitating an interactive networking event:

> *I've been reading your blog and checking out your Web site. I really think you would be a great speaker at our events, and that our members will really identify with you! I love the bits about Facebook in there—I know I'm not the only thirty-something in our group who is still a little baffled by that whole phenomenon. I also signed up for your e-zine and the first e-mail of your 7-day course just showed up in my inbox. Great job!!*

Although she had never met me or heard me speak before, through the content she found on my blog, she got a good sense of my tone and personality and felt that I would be a good fit for her group. We chatted on the phone briefly about the event details and had the contract signed a few days later. The event was so successful that the organization's Connecticut chapter invited me to facilitate its networking event two months later.

Networking gravity is about being smart about *where* you network and *how* you network, incorporating online tools as appropriate, to maximize your chances of making connections with the best fit. That's not to say that you won't want to meet people serendipitously. I do it all the time. When I'm at a conference to speak (point 1 on the list) or attending an event to meet a specific individual (point 2), I'll always try to talk to as many other people as I can while I'm there, and I'll offer help when I'm able to.

Recently, I attended a media breakfast to support a friend who was running the event and met a woman who was starting a niche social networking site for teens. Ten minutes later, I happened to be speaking with a social networking consultant, and I immediately introduced the two. Taking the opportunity when you're networking to connect people who can help each other adds to your networking gravity, because when you initiate a bond between two people, you strengthen the bonds you have with each of them individually.

Captivate Connections through Content and Community

Good networking skills are essential to building networking gravity. You have to know how to act and react appropriately when connecting with others in every type of networking situation, whether it's reaching out to people you already know or making new contacts at events or in networking groups. But those skills will get you only so far because networking one-to-one and hunting down every opportunity yourself is time-consuming.

Content-based marketing like speaking and e-zines (e.g., electronic magazines or newsletters) can turbocharge your networking by allowing your expertise to become known to larger audiences and help you stay top of mind on an ongoing, one-to-many basis. Blogs and social networking sites work 24/7 to allow more people to find you and help you build a worldwide base of connections.

These are the tools that open your door to the world and that allow prospective contacts to learn about you. They will be able to see what you know and understand what opportunities might interest you, whether it's a new job or a new business idea. And when you hear from them, they're already primed to work with you.

My blog, my e-zine, and my profiles on Facebook, LinkedIn, and other social networking sites are networking on my behalf 24/7 worldwide. Harnessing the power of these tools will help to increase your networking gravity, keeping people in your orbit, and attracting more people toward you who want to be part of your universe. They're your support system and independent sales force, bringing opportunities to you and allowing you to reach your goals faster. You'll never have an excuse not to network because you just can't fit it in or just can't get out to networking events.

Sheilah Etheridge lives in Anchorage, Alaska, but through her participation in LinkedIn, she's gained new clients for her accounting and business management consulting firm, and she has been interviewed by various blogs and podcasts all over the world, as well as by *Money* magazine. She contributes frequently to the LinkedIn community by answering questions posed by other members. "All of these things get my name out there and bring inquiries from new people. I help promote others in my network as well. Whenever possible I suggest someone I know in the Q&A forum and have seen those connections get business from it. I have suggested people connect to a particular person and seen them hired for a new job as a result. This is the only place where you can find millions of members all willing to help one another and share freely of their knowledge."

Networking gravity works 24/7 just like regular gravity. It's a concept that every busy professional should master. If you have the right systems in place, you can wake up in the morning to new queries from recruiters, prospects, or potential business partners wanting to work with you. You won't have to constantly search for opportunities, they'll find you from all points around the world.

The Interconnectedness of Process, Preparation, and Purpose

Networking isn't a onetime event or a series of random activities; it's a process. That's right, a process—a sequence of logical steps to follow to get a certain result. If you think of networking that way, you'll be able to get more done in less time with less effort because you'll always know what you have to do next and you won't skip important steps inadvertently.

In my workshops I teach a simple three-step process for networking: prepare, connect, and strengthen. Before you start connecting with anybody either at an event or online, you need to prepare by asking yourself these important questions:

- Whom do I want to meet? What's the best way to meet them?
- What's the best way to introduce myself?
- What questions will I ask?

Many people underestimate the power of preparation in maximizing their networking efforts. Even this simple bit of preparation will make connecting much easier. It will give you a sense of direction that will not only make you feel more at ease but also leave a strong impression of both your competence and your confidence. That's a heck of a lot better than looking lost and uneasy.

A common mistake, and certainly the mistake I made that night at the 21 Club, is to try to go straight into connecting mode. I showed up at that event with absolutely no preparation. I had no clear purpose for attending, no elevator pitch ready, no idea who was going to be there, no idea whom I wanted to meet, and no idea what I would say to them even if I did meet them. No wonder it was a disaster. I thought showing up was good enough. Well, it's not.

It's been said that opportunity happens when luck meets preparation. Showing up is about luck, being at the right place at the right time. But that's only half the equation. Being ready to shine when the spotlight grabs you is about preparation. It's preparation that gives you the confidence to walk into a crowded room. It's preparation that gives you the confidence to start meaningful conversations with strangers. It's preparation that gives you the confidence to offer help to others when they need it and to ask for what you want as well.

Preparation facilitates connection, which in turn, makes the rest of the process of following up and strengthening initial bonds a breeze. Thinking about networking as this three-step process is helpful because no matter what your skill with networking now, you can easily figure out where you can improve. If you're completely new to networking, the process gives you a logical starting point. If you're actively participating but not getting the results you're looking for, you can work through each of the steps in order to pinpoint where you might be having trouble. If you're an expert networker already, you can challenge yourself to streamline each step and find ways to work even smarter.

What drives the entire process is our purpose. When you have a specific goal you're trying to reach, it's much easier to identify whom to connect with, where to connect with them, and what to say. Purpose is the wind in our sails. Without it, we don't have clear direction about where we want to go, and we just drift with the current.

CHAPTER 3

BE FOUND, BE PERSONABLE, BE CREDIBLE

GETTING THE HELP YOU NEED
BECAUSE OF THE PERSON YOU ARE

> Leadership: the art of getting someone else to do something
> you want done because he wants to do it.
>
> —*Dwight D. Eisenhower*

What's important for getting ahead in life has evolved.

- It used to be: It's not *what* you know, but *who* you know.
- Then it became: It's not who you know, but *who knows you*.
- But I believe: It's not who knows you, but *who's willing to help you*.

As much as we'd like to help everyone who asks, we can't. Or we don't. How do we choose, consciously or unconsciously, whom to make that phone call for or give that referral to or approach with a new business opportunity? There's always an underlying reason.

According to Tim Sanders of Yahoo!, likability has a lot to do with it. In *The Likeability Factor: How to Boost Your L-Factor and Achieve Your*

Life's Dreams, he writes that likable people have an easier time getting what they want. His premise is that our lives are determined by the choices others make for us. We don't choose the best job or the best spouse; they choose us. "The more likable you are, the more likely you are to be on the receiving end of a positive choice from which you can profit."

Getting help in networking requires cooperation from others, and the choice to give us that cooperation is theirs. As Tim says, a high L-factor is important. I've found in my own experience that people are more willing to help you if they like you. Before you can get their help, however, you'll need to show up on their radar screens. They need to know who you are and what you do. And before you can get their best help, they need to trust you. Few people will put their businesses on the line to partner with you or risk their reputations recommending you for a big opportunity if they don't think you'll do a good job, even if you're a likable person. So it's not just about likability. Being known and being trusted are equally important.

How do you get there? Sometimes it comes from the word of another person you've already won over. Sometimes it happens all at once at the very first meeting, and you just click. Sometimes it happens in stages over time.

NETWORKING SUCCESS STORY 2
TURNING CHANCE ENCOUNTERS
INTO LIFELONG SUPPORTERS
Bret Allan, Senior Director of Risk Management
Luminant
Dallas, Texas

During his "road warrior" days of consulting, Bret Allan sat next to a guy on a plane named John. They started chatting, and Bret noticed that John was asking really good, probing questions about his background. Bret gave him two hours' worth of advice on why his alma mater, the University of Chicago, would be a great choice for his MBA.

Flash forward to four years later. Bret joined Luminant (then TXU) and was back at the University of Chicago for a recruiting trip. John happened to pass by and reintroduced himself. It turns out that John took Bret's advice and was now an MBA student looking for a job! Since John had no energy experience, he wasn't a fit, but they decided to keep in touch because they found it so humorous how they crossed paths again.

Four years after that, John was working in Richmond, Virginia, but was looking to make a move to Dallas. He saw a job posting at TXU and called Bret to learn more about it. Recognizing that John was a great match for the job based on both work experience and cultural fit, Bret recommended him to the hiring manager, and he is now employed there. "We go to lunch regularly, and he always asks me what I am going to do next, since odds are, he will follow along a few years later!"

Be Known: Are You Registering on Their Radar Screens?

Getting known is important in networking because people have to know who you are before they'll consider doing business with you. Once you've gotten their attention, then you can work on demonstrating your likability and gaining their trust. But you'll never get to that point until you hit their radar. How do you get the process started?

1. Getting Known Face-to-Face

As soon as you introduce yourself to someone in person, you're known. If you're able to have a meaningful conversation, even if just for a few minutes, you can also become liked, and perhaps be on your way to gaining trust as well. It all depends on what you talk about. If you focus on small talk, which is fine for a start, you can build some rapport, but if you're able to turn the conversation to a topic that's important to the people you're talking to, you can get a lot further. Ask about what they do and what brings them to the event, and you'll start to build a much deeper connection. When you can learn more about each other, what you have in common, and where you might be able to contribute to each other's success, you can get on the road toward building trust. Face-to-face meetings can help speed up the process and make subsequent interactions productive.

2. Spreading Your Message through Word of Mouth

My longest-running consulting client came to me through word of mouth shortly after 9/11. While I was on my way to a lunch appointment, I got a call on my cell phone from a gentleman named Jeff Barasch. He was looking for some ongoing help with his company,

Onward Publishing, and I came highly recommended by a friend and former coworker of his, Dennis, whom I had worked with a few years earlier. I met Jeff for lunch the next day and had the contract by the time the lunch check arrived. Apparently, Dennis had given me such a strong recommendation that Jeff was pretty much sold by the time we met. And we're still working together today. As Jeff would say, "Such long-term associations forge mutual respect where both parties benefit."

Word of mouth is a powerful way to get known because it also starts the ball rolling very quickly toward your gaining people's trust. It's important to give your contacts a very clear idea of what you are looking for to ensure that they spread the word to the right people. In *Endless Referrals*, Bob Burg suggests being prepared to answer the question, "How can I know if someone I'm talking to is a good prospect for you?" Even if you aren't asked it directly, you can incorporate it into any conversation you have about your business to give people a clear understanding of what you do and who might interest you as a prospect. It's also a question you should be asking of the people you meet so that you can be sure the referrals you send are appropriate.

3. Being Found Online

Why should you care about making yourself known online for networking purposes? To take advantage of a phenomenon known as the "long tail." Chris Anderson, author of *The Long Tail: Why the Future of Business Is Selling Less of More*, describes it as the collection of product niches in a market outside the mainstream hits that are still in demand by consumers, albeit in smaller numbers. With physical limitations on shelf space, Anderson argues, brick-and-mortar retailers have to focus on carrying the bestsellers. However, we all have interests outside of what's most popular. Those are the products that fall into the long tail of the distribution curve.

Technology innovations have made serving the long tail possible in many industries including music, books, and movies. According to Anderson's research, the average Borders bookstore stocks 100,000 titles. In contrast, Amazon stocks 3.7 million titles, with 25 percent of sales coming from the millions of titles that Borders does not stock. In other words, there's a big market for the niches, not just the blockbusters. I've certainly bought books on Amazon that my local Barnes &

Noble didn't carry, and many of these books I wouldn't even have known about without Amazon's helpful recommendation and search tools.

I believe there is a long tail in networking as well. While you'll spend most of your energy and get the most opportunities from a small percentage of people in your network, other opportunities will come out of the blue from distant contacts who are searching for people in their target niche.

Technology makes it easy for us not just to be found—we've moved beyond the basic information of a telephone directory—but to be *known* to a great many more people, without incremental cost or effort on our part or theirs. Anyone interested in us can read our Web sites, blogs, and online profiles to get a better understanding of who we are. In a sense, we're always "in stock" and available to network without leaving our homes. People will seek us out based on our profile characteristics and some may even bring business opportunities to our door. They may not always be the right opportunities, and we can politely decline, but without the technology that enables this aggregation of people, and a user-friendly way to sort through these folks based on qualifications, interests, and experiences, we'd never even be considered. Just as in any contest, while entering doesn't guarantee you'll win, you certainly can't win if you don't enter.

Our online presence makes us available to network with others and vice versa, at any time of the day or night, from any part of the world at low cost. You don't know where opportunities will come from, but it doesn't take any more time or energy to be found by 5 million people than by 5 people. In addition, these online communities can help fill needs that you may have as well. If you're looking for new business partners, customers, or employees, these same channels can help you find them, and possibly vet them.

Be Liked: Are You Playing Your Strongest Rapport Card?

While working in the San Francisco office of Booz & Company (back then known as Booz Allen Hamilton) after business school, I was assigned to a project for several months in the New York City office. Every day, on the walk from my corporate apartment, I would pick up a cinnamon raisin bagel for breakfast at a deli that made them on site and often served them warm. I was always friendly to the man behind the counter, greeting him with a hello, and making my bagel request with a smile.

One day when I got to the deli, I found that it had run out of cinnamon bagels, but as it turns out, the man behind the counter had set aside the last one for me. It was waiting already wrapped up and ready to go. Every so often the cinnamon bagels would sell out early, but I knew there was always one waiting just for me.

Being likable gets you more than the last bagel in life. It's also essential in networking because it draws people in, makes them comfortable with you, and lowers their defenses. They're relaxed and more open, making it easier to build a connection.

1. Building Rapport Face-to-Face

I was facilitating a networking event in Connecticut and met Marc, one of the participants, during dinner. I was struck by how he was able to engage each person around him one by one, getting people to talk by asking thoughtful questions, paying attention to them as they answered, and offering helpful but not forceful advice. A number of people I spoke to later remarked that although they're introverts, Marc got them out of their shell. He was indeed a very likable guy.

Within a few minutes of meeting someone, you can often sense whether or not you'll like him and want to get to know him better. Does he smile easily? Does he seem to treat the people around him with respect? Is he pleasant to be around? Does he seem interested in you?

You can also tell fairly quickly if you're not going to like someone. Is he overbearing? Is he critical? Is he full of himself? If you don't like him, you won't want to spend much time with him. And while first impressions can sometimes be wrong, you're more likely to move on than to stick around to give this person a second chance.

2. Building Rapport Online

While meeting in person can give you a quick impression, you can also get a strong sense of people's personality and potential likability by what you see about them online, on their blogs and social networking profiles. Is their profile interesting? Does their picture show warmth and friendliness? Do you have things in common? Do you like what they say and how they say it?

If you're being considered for a potential opportunity—a new job, a new contract, a new project—how you present yourself online could be one of the first ways people will assess whether they like you enough to take you to the next stage. So get yourself in the game by making sure that whatever information is available about you online puts you in a favorable light.

Be Trusted: Are You Offering Tangible Proof?

In *The Speed of Trust: The One Thing That Changes Everything*, Stephen M. R. Covey sums up the economics of trust this way: by increasing trust, you increase speed and decrease costs. Conversely, low trust leads to low speed and higher costs. Trust is important in networking because in order to get things for yourself and for others, you need to engage people who are willing to go the extra mile for you. Gaining trust and keeping it should be a priority in all your relationships. How do you develop it in the first place?

1. Trust Can Be *Initiated* by Your Keeping Your Promises

When people meet you for the first time having no prior knowledge of you, how do you gain their trust? Little things can make a big difference, like being on time for meetings. That sends a strong signal that you're someone who honors your commitments. And following through on a simple promise such as sending information you said you'd send or making a phone call you said you'd make also demonstrates that you respect them.

2. Trust Can Be *Experienced* by Your Doing Good Work

If you've done a good job for people in the past, they're more likely to trust that you'll do a good job again in the future. Additionally, they're more likely to trust you for a bigger job if you've performed well on a smaller job. This is probably the highest level of trust you can gain because the proof is in the pudding. They've seen your performance with their own eyes. You promised, and you delivered.

3. Trust Can Be *Transferred* through Your Connections

When you ask someone you trust for a recommendation, whether for a restaurant, dentist, or vendor, you'll often put a higher level of faith in the person they recommend than you would in someone you pick randomly from the phone book. In other words, if you trust Joe, and Joe trusts Margaret, then you will start off with trusting Margaret more than you would the average person on the street.

That's why trust gained through experience is so important. If people have a good experience with you, they are more likely to recommend you to others, giving you a leg up on the competition. Remember though that if you look good, your connector will look good. If you look bad, your connector will look bad. For that very reason, when someone asks you for a recommendation, it's important that you are 100 percent comfortable with whom you refer.

4. Trust Can Be *Conveyed* through Your Expertise

As much as we probably hate to admit it, we tend to put a lot of trust in experts. That's why people work so hard and pay so much money to acquire those fancy letters after their names. It enhances their credibility. When you share your knowledge through writing or public speaking, you're given expert status over the people in your field who don't do those things. And we tend to trust experts, at least as it relates to their subject area, even when we know nothing else about them.

Gaining Trust Online

As more avenues become available for people to find information about you, through blogs and social networking especially, the easier it becomes for them to decide whether or not to trust you without ever having to interact with you directly. Not only can you present an enormous amount of evidence to make your case, but you can also reach a massive audience in the same amount of time it would take to reach just one person offline.

NETWORKING SUCCESS STORY 3
GAINING TRUST WITH A MOUNTAIN OF EVIDENCE
Patsi Krakoff and Denise Wakeman
The Blog Squad
Southern California

Patsi and Denise, a.k.a. The Blog Squad, have been blogging since September 2004 and use business blogs to target three primary niches of online marketing for the small business professional.

When they started, they had no idea what would happen, but they soon found that their revenues had quadrupled and their mailing list had grown tenfold. They are well known and highly regarded in their niche; they contributed chapters to several books on e-mail marketing, blogging, and e-commerce, participated in a live Webcast for Wells Fargo Small Business; and they get invitations nearly every week to speak at conferences. They've also been interviewed by the *Wall Street Journal* and local area TV, as well as Japanese TV and newspapers and on Internet radio and podcasts.

They fell in love with blogging for many reasons. For one, blogging is inexpensive and easy to do, which means that Patsi and Denise don't have to rely on a Web designer; they can tweak and update their blogs themselves. One thing that they didn't expect was the amazing networking benefits of business blogging.

Patsi and Denise say that they are a couple of introverts who prefer to avoid breakfast meetings. They use their blogs to network and to connect with prospects and colleagues with like values and interests. A single blog post can resonate with a reader who may then invite them to speak at a conference or be on a radio show, or hire them to help with his or her business. "Writing on our blogs several times a week, and commenting on other blogs, is like having an open phone line to a global audience. We get e-mail and phone calls from people all over the world we wouldn't have otherwise met."

Networking through blogging has all the value of local networking without the travel and bad breakfasts. And it can do so much more; Patsi and Denise have ongoing meaningful, global conversations that result in more opportunities than they ever imagined.

PART II

CONNECTING ONE-TO-ONE

STRENGTHENING YOUR CORE SKILLS AND RELATIONSHIPS

CHAPTER 4

WIND UP FOR THE PITCH

PRESENTING YOURSELF WITH CLARITY AND CONVICTION

> I care not what others think of what I do,
> but I care very much about what I think of what I do. That is character!
>
> —*Theodore Roosevelt*

"So, what do you do?" One of the most important preparation steps you can take in networking before you get out and start connecting with others is to formulate a strong answer to this question.

Of all the topics in the world to talk about, talking about ourselves should be the easiest, and therefore this question should be a slam dunk, right? Wrong. Few people manage to answer this question effectively. Some don't like their work or don't want to be defined by it so they share very little. Others can't wait to be asked this question so that they can launch into a 10-minute commercial about their latest product breakthrough, complete with handouts.

Then there are those who just seem to freeze. "I never know what to say." "It seems so canned." "What I do is so boring, nobody would be interested." So they string a few phrases together, full of industry jargon and devoid of coherent thought, and then hastily swing the spotlight to a more neutral subject.

Why does this happen? Two reasons. First, since we do our jobs 8 to 12 hours or more a day, this is a question we feel we should be able to answer off the cuff, so we never take the time to prepare a strong response. Only when we start talking do we realize how difficult it really is to encapsulate what we do in a sound bite. So as we're speaking out loud, our inner monologue is silently dubbing over our words: "Of course I know what I do, and it should be easy for me to talk about it. The fact that I'm struggling is probably telling this guy that I'm not good at what I do, and that is killing me because I know I am fabulous. Why is this so hard? He's squinting at me and not getting what I'm saying. Oh no, I'm totally losing him. There. I'm finished, and I'm changing the subject. Cue the spotlight."

We act surprised, as if the question came out of left field, even though we've been asked it many times before in the same situations and will undoubtedly be asked it many times more. Yet few of us are prepared for this inevitability.

The second reason we falter is that we don't realize how important this question is in building the foundation of a relationship. Connections happen through conversation, and in many environments where people are meeting one another for business, asking "What do you do?" is a way of initiating conversation that starts the connection process.

Of course, outside of a business setting, asking "What do you do?" might be considered impolite as a first question. Like at yoga class or in church or at your aunt's tea party. However, even in purely social situations, the question may come up. It's a mechanism most of us have learned to use to open up the lines of communication, giving someone permission to share something about themselves. So when it's asked of you, why not strive to sound as engaged and engaging as you possibly can? You never know where it can lead. But you have to do it in the right way. You can answer to get yourself off the hot seat, or you can answer to draw listeners in.

While people are listening for the content of your answer by *what* you're saying, they're also unconsciously evaluating other key criteria for a relationship by *how* you're saying it. They're forming their first impressions of you with this first interaction by silently assessing:

- Is this person interesting?
- Is she someone I should get to know better?
- Does she have knowledge or skills that can help me or someone I know?
- Is there any way that I can help her?

Engaging in conversation is the only way to complete this assessment. Not all these questions will occur to everyone. Effective networkers will stay with the conversation long enough to get all four questions answered, though they may jump around. The most generous networkers will unconsciously start their wheels turning with the last question and work backwards to the other questions. Uncertain networkers, those with no clear purpose for being at an event, will probably start and stop at the first question, not knowing where to go next and hoping the other person will pick up the slack in the conversation.

Of course, you're doing your own assessment once it's your turn to ask, "What do you do?" How each of you responds will determine whether you'll eagerly arrange to follow up after the event to continue the discussion in more depth or whether you'll just kill time with idle banter. With so much riding on this one question, shouldn't we spend just a little time crafting an answer that can help us move the relationship forward?

All is not lost if you don't rattle off a completely captivating answer; it's still possible to make a great connection depending on your personality and the other person's patience. But why handicap yourself? It's not that hard to construct a compelling introduction. You just have to know what to do and then make time to get it done.

It's time to wind up for the pitch.

Actually, It's More Like Catch

Your introduction, also known as an elevator pitch, is a key component for networking. An elevator pitch is a way of talking about yourself that is informative, inviting, and intriguing. It's called an elevator pitch because it should be short, something you can say within the span of time it takes for an elevator to get from one floor to another, usually no more than 10 to 15 seconds. I also like to think that in an ideal world, your elevator pitch would be so persuasive that it would cause the person you're talking to to miss his or her floor completely in order to hear more. It's something to strive for, anyway.

While your introduction is known as a pitch, it's more like a friendly game of catch. You're not throwing the ball as hard as you can to knock the person over. You're actually tossing it gently so that it can be caught and thrown back to you, keeping the ball in play with gentle underhand throws as you converse back and forth.

Don't go in with the expectation that you can close a sale with your pitch. You'll end up being too wordy, looking too aggressive, or sounding too desperate. And you'll repel rather than attract someone you may want to get to know. You can't build a relationship with someone who doesn't want to be around you. Your goal with your pitch is not to sell, but simply to generate interest in who you are and to hint at the value you can bring. Your message may not connect with everyone because of a mismatch of interests, professions, or temperaments, but if you're in front of someone you should have in your network, that person will keep the ball in play by continuing the conversation to find out more.

Create a Standard, but Include Some Range

What goes into your pitch will depend on your networking objectives. What's your overall goal? You'll have a different pitch if you're networking to win new clients for your business rather than networking to change careers. In the first instance you'll highlight the types of clients you serve and the benefits you offer. In the second, you'll talk less about your current profession and more about what you need to pursue your new path.

Who's your audience? Your pitch might change depending on the situation and whom you're speaking with. You may emphasize a different aspect of your company in your pitch if you're recruiting new hires rather than if you're going to a venture capital conference to find investors. You also might give a different pitch in a social situation than you would at an industry trade show.

Have a few pitches in your back pocket ready to go at any time. And before you attend any important networking events and meetings, make sure you prepare exactly what you're going to say. In the following section, we'll work out the elements of an appropriate pitch using a sample scenario of attracting new business opportunities at a networking event. You can find samples for other networking scenarios, such as finding a job or changing careers, at www.smartnetworking.com.

The Multilayered Pitch: Ready for One or All

The ideal way to deliver a pitch when you're speaking to someone one-on-one is through conversation. Again, think of that game of catch. You share a little something, the person you're playing with shares a little something, you share a little more, and so on. Tossing the ball back and forth through questions.

NETWORKER: "Hello, I'm Jim Martin."

ME: "Hi, Liz Lynch."

NETWORKER: "So what do you do?"

ME: "I teach people how to network smart. What about you?"

NETWORKER: "Well, I've been in the real estate business for 15 years, mostly on the commercial side."

ME: "Oh? What types of clients do you work with?"(keeping the ball on his side)

NETWORKER: Mainly retail clients trying to find new locations for their stores. How long have you been involved with teaching networking?" (tossing the ball back to me)

When you're addressing a group with your pitch, which may happen at certain networking events, you can reveal more of your pitch all at once: "I'm Jim Martin. I'm in the commercial real estate business, specializing in helping retail clients find the best locations for their new stores." In this case, it's even more important to craft your pitch carefully so the elements flow together.

Think of your pitch not as one big chunk, but as a set of blocks that you can configure in different ways depending on the situation. There will be a first foundational level that you'll use all the time and then other levels that can build from there. Here's a set of questions to cover every level that you should be prepared to answer before you start connecting. The more prepared you are, the more you can focus on the conversation and not get caught up in what you should say next, or worse, what you should have said, but didn't.

The First Level: The Basic Coordinates

These are the questions you'll get asked up front whether you're speaking with an individual or addressing a group. They're fairly basic, but you can still get some mileage from your answers if you know how to handle them. Answering both should take less than five seconds. Once I attended an event where someone gave about eight different company names she was involved with. I stopped listening after the fourth one, and by the time she was done with the eighth, I had forgotten the first three. Better to stick with one answer.

"What's Your Name?"

You may be used to saying your name, but few people are used to hearing it. Be sure you say it clearly and slowly, especially in a group setting. In front of a group you should also be prepared to say your company name, especially if the company you work for is well known (people like to grab onto something familiar) or if you run your own business (a bit of free marketing for you). More and more, I've been saying my company URL instead of the company name to make it even easier for people to look me up online later if they don't get a chance to speak with me in person. So I'll say, "Hi, I'm Liz Lynch of NetworkingExcellence.com," which is shorter than "Hi, I'm Liz Lynch from the Center for Networking Excellence." To avoid sounding like a commercial, pick one or the other, don't say both.

"What Do You Do?"

The essence of what you do should be condensed into a one-line tagline. One line will make it easier for people to remember. Recently I attended a two-day seminar in San Francisco and had a chance to share my tagline, "I teach people how to network smart." When speaking to a large group, people don't always remember faces, but they may catch bits of words here and there, especially if they connect with the message. During the breaks and at the cocktail party that evening, when people asked me what I do I would once again give them my one-line tagline. When I did that, they remembered me immediately. A few even said to me, "Oh, great. I wanted to speak to you because what you said is something I need."

Now, I could have said, I'm a consultant, or an author, or a speaker, but that would have gotten lost because it's too generic. People would have heard it and forgotten it instantly or would have confused me with others in the room who were consultants, authors, or speakers. The one-line tagline differentiates you at the same time that it generates interest—others want to learn more.

The Second Level: The Additional Hooks

Second-level questions are follow-ups that people have a chance to ask you during a conversation in order to understand more deeply what you do. If you have a chance to introduce yourself to a group, it may be appropriate to add one of these to your first-level answers. Keep your answers to each question to 10 seconds or less. If people really want more detail, they'll find you afterward. It's always better not to over-stay your welcome.

"What Brings You Here?"

What are you looking for? What's your objective for attending the event? It doesn't have to be a big reason. If you're there simply to learn and get inspired, then say that. If you're there to meet specific types of people, who are they? This question gives others the opportunity to understand your most immediate needs and assess whether they can help you or know someone who can. It can be a quick win-win for both of you if they can find a way to help.

At that seminar in San Francisco, one of my primary objectives was to find marketing partners for this book, which I shared with one gentleman. Immediately, he said, "Have you met Ruby? She does multimedia e-books that help authors drive sales of their physical books." In fact, I hadn't met Ruby, but made it a point to find her at the next break, and I subsequently learned of an opportunity that I definitely wanted to be a part of. Had I not articulated my goal for attending the event, I might never have gotten that spot-on recommendation.

"Who's Your Ideal Prospect?"

Nailing down a concise answer to this question can be a challenge. Many people tend to say, "Anybody and everybody" which is not a great response, and here's why. We may hit it off in our first conversation and I'll want to find a way to help you, but you have to connect the dots for me. If you can't give me a specific client profile, I won't be able to rifle through my mental database of contacts to pick someone out for you as a referral. And I'm not going to choose someone randomly. I have too much respect for the members of my network to tie up their time with a possible wild-goose chase. So you need to narrow down the field. What size companies do you work with? What's the title of the person who typically hires you? Do you specialize by industry or geography?

I realize that many business owners and salespeople are skittish about getting too specific about their prospect because they feel it will narrow their market too much and they'll miss out on referrals. That's why they say, "Anybody and everybody." To give some direction but also leave the door open, you might say, "I work with many different types of clients, but most of my work lately has been with professional service firms." Or, "My clients are pretty diverse, but I really enjoy working with women business owners, especially after they've reached the $10 million mark in revenues."

Again, all you're trying to do is give a succinct but detailed description of your ideal customer, almost as if you're describing a picture to a police sketch artist, so that it's easier for someone to find that customer for you.

The Third Level: The Juicy Details

The next set of questions falls into another level of information, which people might ask if they're interested in your services or have a lot of time to spend with you. Think of all those times you've sat next to someone at lunch and needed to fill up the time—that's where these third-level questions can move the conversation forward in a productive manner.

"Why Do They Come to You?"

This question asks about the needs of your prospect. In other words, "How can I recognize when someone should contact you?" You can describe a common problem that your ideal customer faces and how your product or service can address it. Your answer to this question can be another way contacts can help pinpoint the perfect referral for you from all the people they know.

"Why Do They Choose You?"

In other words, why would someone buy from you? What's your key point of differentiation? Think carefully about this because it should be a characteristic that your ideal customer cares about and is also a true point of differentiation for you, something that your competitors do not offer. Some important differentiators could be a deep knowledge of the industry or level of personal service. This is the time to highlight something special about you and your company that would make someone feel good about referring a friend or colleague to you. A differentiator could also be price, although that is a tricky competitive advantage to claim if you don't have the volume or operational capability to sustain lower prices. It doesn't make sense to win against your competitors if you have to go broke in the process.

"Can You Give Me an Example?"

Or, "How do you do that?" This is your time to tell a story to help bring your pitch to life. Prepare a few different stories in advance so that you can choose the one most likely to resonate with the person you're speaking with. Here's how it would go:

> NETWORKER: "Can you give me a typical example of a client you worked with?"
>
> YOU: "Sure. You said you were in pharmaceutical sales, right?"
>
> NETWORKER: "Yes, that's right."
>
> YOU: "Well, recently I worked with a health-care company that . . ."

If you give an example in an industry or in a situation that the other person can relate to, your story will be easier to grasp and remember. When crafting your story, set up the situation in a couple of sentences, describe briefly what you did, and then outline the key benefits your client received.

"If I'm Interested in Your Services, What Should I Do Next?"

This question tees up your call to action, though in most cases it will rarely be served up to you so nicely. Still, you want to have a response ready should you get the question in a conversation, and just as important, you want to be able to weave it into any pitch you give to a group so the information is out there. Here are a couple of examples:

- "I'm happy to talk to you more about your technology challenges and see if there's a way we can help. Why don't I take your card and give you a call tomorrow?"
- "The first place to start is to download our free report at our Web site which describes what to look for when hiring a branding company, and what it's like to work with us in particular. If that sounds good to you, then give me a call. Here's my direct line."

A call to action gives those listening to your pitch clear directions about next steps, carefully laying down the cobblestones so the path to the resolution of all of their problems leads directly to you, if there's a fit, of course. The next steps might be so obvious to you that you'd think you'd hardly need to spell them out for anyone. However, because all of us have so much on our minds that when we can be gently guided somewhere and not have to think too much, we'll often follow readily.

When giving your pitch to a group, insert your call to action at the end. Continuing with the example we started earlier in the chapter: "I'm Jim Martin. I'm in the commercial real estate business, specializing in helping retail clients find the best locations for their new stores. If you or anyone you know has a retail business that is expanding and wants to work with someone who knows this market inside and out, I'd welcome the opportunity to speak with you at the break, or you can visit our Web site at jimmartinrealestate.com for more information."

Being aware of the range of questions that people might ask to get to know you better will help you prepare more concise, compelling, and complete answers than if you had to think off the cuff. You have time to think about how to position yourself in the best light and generate interest.

Use these questions yourself in conversations with others, to draw them out, help you connect with them more effectively, and understand better what they do and how you might be able to help. They'll think you're a brilliant conversationalist even if they do all the talking!

In terms of time limits, your story or example could be anywhere from 30 to 60 seconds, while your other answers will be shorter. Again, you can always go into much more detail if it's appropriate. Detail isn't hard. Being concise is. But forcing yourself to be concise will make it easier for your listeners to digest answers, and that's the most important thing. Remember, it's not about what you say but what others are able to understand and take away that matters most.

Have your business card ready to give out, but not until the end of the conversation or when someone asks for it, whichever comes first. You'll be more effective when you hand out your card as a natural wrap up to the conversation rather than the lead into it. You want the person to focus on getting to know you as a person, not you as a 2-inch by 3.5-inch piece of card stock.

Believe in Your Pitch or No One Else Will

Crafting a clear and compelling pitch is an investment. Woodrow Wilson was once asked how long it took him to write a speech. He said, "That depends. If I am to speak 10 minutes, I need a week. If 15 minutes, three days. If half an hour, two days. If an hour, I am ready now."

Delivering an unfocused pitch with no preparation will save you time now, but you'll lose that time on the back end of your networking because it will take longer for the right people to find you. It's much more productive to put the time in up front.

1. *Work out the key messages first.*   Before you agonize over the exact words, figure out what you want the gist of your message to be. A friend of mine was planning a trip to Mexico to meet his girlfriend's family for the first time. He told me that the family didn't speak much English, but he knew they would probably ask him about his intentions for the relationship and he needed to figure out how to communicate that in Spanish. I laughed, and said, "Well, before you worry about your Spanish, maybe you

should first figure out what your answer would be in English." In your pitch, which of your services will you emphasize? What are your best stories and examples? How do those highlight your unique qualities?

2. *Go back and replace jargon and buzzwords with real words.* Even though the phrase "usability testing algorithms" might look good on paper, not only is that a mouthful to say, but few people will understand what it is. The more highly specialized vocabulary you use, the smaller the market will be of people who will understand what you're talking about and be able to help you. All because of a few buzzwords. What a waste. If you can explain in lay terms what you do, or better yet, if you can explain to a fifth grader what you do (e.g., "I help companies build Web sites that make it easier for users to find what they're looking for"), more people will understand it and, in turn, be able to tell others about you. If they can't understand what you do, they won't be able to bring you any further into their network.

3. *Rehearse your pitch until you can say it smoothly.* Say it out loud to yourself several times. Start off by reading it straight off the page or computer screen. If you find yourself tripping over any words, come up with different ones. Time yourself and follow the guidelines I suggested. The first part of your pitch—first and second levels—should go no longer than 15 seconds total. Otherwise it will sound like a monologue, and people will get bored and stop listening. You want to stop at a point where it would be natural for someone to say, "How do you do that?" or ask another question. As an extra step, you can record yourself pitching into a digital recorder to check for speed and the tone of your voice. Make sure you're infusing energy and inflection into your voice and not speaking in a monotone.

4. *Practice your pitch in front of real people.* One of the reasons to attend networking events is to practice your pitch in front of others and see how they react to it. Or split test two different pitches and see which one gets a better response. What you think is clear might still include language that 95 percent of business professionals do not understand. If people ask you, "What's a CMO?" or "What's strategic planning?" you need to describe the concepts in a different way. Also, what you think is compelling

might illicit yawns or skeptical looks. Or if you hear, "How is that different from what Company XYZ does?" then you haven't clearly hit a differentiation point.

5. *Listen for how others might describe you.*   You may learn a different, and perhaps more effective, way to describe yourself. As an example, the women in one of my networking groups used to host regular wine and cheese get-togethers which were more relaxed and covered more personal ground than our business-oriented monthly meetings. Gayle was attending for the first time and was describing to Carey that she helps people with their financial planning needs. Carey, a branding expert, said, "Oh, you're a private wealth advisor." Gayle's face lit up, and she exclaimed, "Yes, I am!" A good pitch is something that is memorable and that others can say on your behalf. If you can use their words, that's even better.

NETWORKING SUCCESS STORY 4
DECLARING WHAT YOU WANT—AND GETTING IT
Laura Allen, Cofounder
15SecondPitch
New York, New York

How do you pitch yourself if you're not sure exactly what you want to do? It's easy, choose one thing to focus on, and test out your 15SecondPitch.

Laura Allen's client Sara was a twenty-something, shy, yet ambitious graphic designer trying to find a full-time job in New York City. However, after going on several interviews, she knew she wouldn't be happy at any of those companies. She asked for help about what to do next.

Sara had a lot of ideas, but there was one thing she was passionate about—Japan. With Laura's help, they developed her pitch around that theme, and she started going to networking events and telling people about her interest in moving there.

The first person she spoke to was an American who happened to be studying Japanese for fun. They struck up a conversation and had a great time talking about Japanese food and films. She went to more events, shared her pitch with more people, and gained more confidence as she got more and more positive feedback. She also began researching companies that taught English to Japanese students.

After pitching for just a few weeks, Sara noticed that the top company on her list was hosting a large group orientation. She went to the interview armed with the knowledge of what made her better than other candidates, and she got the job.

It was a pretty big culture shock to actually be living in Japan within three months of focusing on this goal, but Sara is enjoying every moment of this unique experience and credits Laura's help with creating a great 15SecondPitch that landed her a dream job abroad.

Make Your Pitch Work for You

The beauty of developing your pitch once and for all is that you can use it in many different places, wherever you have interactions with other people. Your ultimate goal is to create a pitch that is repeatable and that relays your message consistently, whether in condensed or expanded form, throughout all of your marketing. The big test of success is when people are able to explain accurately to others what you do and when that third-party explanation is able to generate attention and interest for you.

1. Serve It Up at Events

At networking events, you should be ready with your strongest pitch targeted to the people you're likely to meet. Be prepared to give your pitch piece by piece in a one-on-one conversation, but there also may be an opportunity to give your pitch to the whole group. Some organizations open their meetings by asking all participants to stand up and introduce themselves.

2. Add It to Marketing Materials

You can also add a short-form version of your pitch as a tagline to your marketing materials. Putting your pitch on your business cards, brochures, and Web sites will reinforce your core message. However, before you spend a lot of money printing or reprinting your marketing collateral, be sure you road test your pitch so that you settle on one that works pretty universally.

3. Transfer It Online

Include a version of your pitch in all your online profiles. Depending on your situation, this could include the About Us page of your Web site and blog, and on your Facebook and LinkedIn pages (more about that in Chapter 12). You might want to expand on your pitch and give more information than you would usually cover in person. You can also excerpt your pitch into a short-form version to use in the signature line of your e-mail.

4. Preface a Question with It

One not-so-obvious place to use your pitch is as a preface to a question you might ask in a public forum. Conferences and other big industry events are target-rich environments for potential customers and business partners, and asking a smart question during the Q&A period of a breakout session is a great place to get noticed. But don't just ask the question. Preface it with a short version of your pitch.

A gentleman I know, whom I'll call Bob, did exactly this at a conference. When the speaker called for questions, Bob raised his hand, stood up and said, "My name is Bob Smith with The Mergers & Acquisitions Company. We help privately held businesses find an exit strategy, and my question is . . .," and then he launched into his question. He said that as soon as the session ended, five people approached him and that he got business from three of them. He never would have found those prospects on his own in the room of 200, so he did something to make them seek *him* out. They self-selected, making his job a lot easier.

You can do the same thing. All it takes is a little prep work to develop the question ahead of time and tie it into your pitch so that you say it effortlessly and easily. Then stand back and watch what happens.

5. Trot It Out for Social Occasions

To pitch or not to pitch at social events? That is the question. My strategy is to be ready with a light version of my pitch, but to hold back unless the conversation seems to be going in that direction. Take your cue from the person you're talking to, and keep it informal even when you're informing. While it could happen that the other person or other guests at the event would fit your target market, you don't want to be "salesy" or come on too strong. This isn't the place for that.

You can use these same guidelines in any informal situation. One Friday I was picking up my morning croissant at a neighborhood bakery and spotted a gentleman whom I usually see only on the weekends paying for his breakfast at the counter. We always said hello to each other but never really had a conversation. That day we chatted for a couple of minutes about why he happened to be in the bakery on a Friday.

He said, "I'm off today because I worked some extra hours during the week. What about you?"

"I work for myself so I'm here every day," I replied.

"Oh? What do you do?" he asked.

Thinking quickly about which pitch to give, strategy consulting or networking, I finally said, "I help media companies develop new revenue streams."

"So you have an MBA?"

"Yes. I went to Stanford, but that was a long time ago."

He chuckled, "I got mine at Columbia, probably before you were even born."

Even in casual environments, people ask what we do because that's a way they can connect with us on neutral territory. Other questions like, "Where do you live?" "Are you married?" "What do you do for fun?" seem a tad too personal for a first conversation. If you want to know something about someone, asking about work is usually safer ground.

The Inside Pitch: Connecting with Colleagues at the Office

Much of this chapter focuses on your outside pitch, what you might say to introduce yourself when meeting a stranger. As I've emphasized, the purpose of asking the "What do you do?" question is to initiate a connection with you, and the purpose of answering it well is to get someone's attention and acknowledge that you're interested in connecting too.

The equivalent to "What do you do?" for people who already know you—friends, coworkers, clients, and business partners—is "What's new?" or "What's going on?" It serves the same purpose in establishing, or rather reestablishing, a connection. It's a way for your colleagues and friends to plug back into your world and your opportunity to articulate something interesting about what you're doing. It's a gift.

Most of the time, however, we don't accept the gift. We simply say, "Things are good. Really busy," and we've missed an opportunity to reinforce a connection with that person, sending the signal that we're not in the mood to play. Our vagueness might be seen as a way to end the conversation—meaning, "I don't have time to tell you more," or "I can't tell you more," and there's nowhere to go from there. Your colleague can end up feeling rebuffed and unimportant, which is not a great way to maintain relationships at the office. Your goal is to inform in an interesting way, but not overwhelm. Give an overview, not a play-by-play.

Here's a framework to help you think about what you might say. First, pick one project you're currently working on, preferably one the other person will find interesting or relevant. Then, home in on an insight or challenge that this project provides. What can you say that is unique, unexpected, or exciting? It could be something that ties into current events, a major initiative of your company, a special challenge that you haven't encountered before, or something that's important to a client. Finally, highlight an opportunity. How does that insight or challenge showcase something about the value you or your employer is providing?

Here's an example from a senior manager at one of my big four accounting clients: "I'm working on the Acme Inc. audit right now. It's interesting because last year there were some issues with Sarbanes-Oxley, but this year they're all buttoned up and we can spend a lot more time on advisory work, which is a lot more fun." Project, insight, and opportunity have all been described in just a couple of sentences.

Your inside pitch should be just this short. Of course, the person may be intrigued and have enough time to ask you for more details, at which time you can share, but resist the temptation to go beyond this initially or you'll risk sounding like a commercial. Your objective is not to brag but to inform. Who knows? The other person might be working on something that's related or be able to provide you with some helpful information.

Be sure to ask about what your colleague is working on as well and give him or her a chance to share something about a current project. Imagine if you could connect with all of your colleagues this way at the office, instead of punting on the question as most people frequently do. Your relationships would be richer and the flow of information more robust.

CHAPTER 5

RECONNECT WITH RAVING FANS

LINING UP SUPPORT FROM YOUR STRONGEST SUPPORTERS

> To be capable of steady friendship or lasting love are the two greatest proofs, not only of goodness of heart, but of strength of mind.
>
> —*William Hazlitt*

When I launched my consulting practice in 2000, my primary business development strategy was to meet with more than a dozen ex-colleagues, friends, and trusted advisors. I was surprised by how easy it was to reconnect with them, some of whom I hadn't spoken to in a few years. All it took was a personal e-mail letting them know I had left corporate America to go out on my own and asking if they had time to catch up over coffee. I was even more surprised by how much of my business that first year came from those few meetings. I never knew my contacts had so much clout!

One of the highest leverage activities you can undertake when starting to network, or even if you're well underway, is to strengthen the connections you already have. When two people haven't interacted in a while, the lines of communication can get clogged. It's like a new pen that's been sitting in a drawer for a while. You know it's full of ink, but you can't get it to write because the ink has settled. Reengaging with contacts is like warming up the pen so the ink can flow again. By warming up the lines of communication, information and help can flow more freely in both directions.

Those who already know, like, and trust you are your strongest allies in networking. They're the people who know you best, who have worked with you before, and who wouldn't hesitate to work with you again. They're the ones who'll give you the strongest recommendations and are comfortable introducing you to just about anyone in their network. They're also the ones most likely to go out of their way to help you. So it makes a lot of sense to start there.

You don't need celebrities in your network. I don't. My network is filled with people who are special to me, but none is a household name or possesses superhuman powers. To me, the secret lies less in *who's* in your network and more in *how* you relate to your network. There's enormous potential with your current contacts. You just have to know how to unlock it.

Remind Me Why We're Friends Again

Before you start reaching out to everyone in your address book, keep in mind a few key guidelines that will increase your chances of getting off on the right foot and getting the help you need.

First, it's important to remember that if you're hoping to leverage a personal relationship with someone, then you should plan to treat that someone very personally. Therefore, no mass e-mails with your résumé or new marketing brochure attached. Or worse, mass e-mails with your résumé or new marketing brochure attached, *and* all your contacts' e-mail addresses listed in the "To:" line for everyone to see. That's a sure way to lose friends very quickly, especially when 45 people hit the "reply all" button to respond back.

Why does that still happen so much? Haven't we all been using e-mail for a while? But I digress.

Second, you want to put some thought into whom you should reconnect with. You don't have to contact everyone in your network. Networking smart is about prioritizing and always linking your actions to your overall goals to get the maximum results. A good place to start is to consider some combination of people who:

- *Do what you do.* As peers you can have candid discussions and get feedback on your goals and plans.
- *Are similar to your target audience with respect to industry and position.* You'll be able to ask questions that get into the mind of your target, such as what challenges are they facing, what are their most pressing needs, and what's the best way to position yourself?
- *Are in high-level positions regardless of industry.* High-level people know other high-level people.
- *Are raving fans of yours no matter what they do.* They will be your biggest cheerleaders, keeping you motivated and feeling good about where you're going. They're also the ones most likely to give you the strongest recommendations, especially if they're familiar with your work.

Third, you don't have to send a formal letter to ask for a meeting. An e-mail or a phone call is just fine. When you do ask for the meeting, be clear about your purpose, for example, that you're headed in a new direction and would like to get their advice, but don't go into too much detail. It's better to wait until you meet in person so you have time to go through the story the way that you want to. And never forget who is doing whom the favor. Always work with their schedule and make meeting times and locations convenient for them.

Conducting the Meeting with Grace

Since you requested the meeting, your contact will look to you to lead it, so have a clear road map in mind. Here's the process I like to follow:

1. Kick Off Casually before Getting Down to Business

It sets a tone for the meeting that is relaxed and informal. Put the focus on them by letting them speak first about their experiences since they last saw you. Ask how things are going, and let them talk about whatever they want, whether it's work-related or personal.

Most people won't talk for more than a few minutes before either finishing up a story or turning the tables to ask what you've been up to. This is your signal to transition to business. You could say something like, "I really appreciate your taking the time to meet. As I mentioned, I'm starting a new business/making a career change/taking my company in a new direction, and since you know a lot about the industry/were able to make the leap yourself/grew your company so dramatically, I wanted to test a few ideas with you and get your opinion on where I'm going."

2. Give Your Pitch and Get Their Opinion

Prepare a variation of your pitch to describe what you're doing, why you're doing it, whom you're targeting, and what help you're looking for. Here's one way to structure it: "Here's the idea. I'm developing a service that [describe a key benefit here]. My goal is to work with [identify the types of companies you're targeting] who need help [describe the types of problems you'll address]. I think there might be a big market there."

Or, if you're looking for a job you might say: "Here's what I'd like to do. I'd like to take my skills in [pick your top two or three strengths] and work with [identify the types of companies you're targeting] that need people who can [describe your unique expertise]. I think that will fit well with what I'm good at and what I like to do."

End your pitch by asking for their feedback. In general, most people want to help when they can and feel bad when they can't. The easiest help you can get is an opinion, so start there. End your pitch with a question like, "What do you think about that? Does that make sense to you?" Often your contacts might add an important twist or ask you to clarify something, which is great feedback for your pitch going forward. They're already helping you just by telling you what they think, and you're getting them more involved with your plans.

3. Lead into "the Ask" Gently

An ideal outcome of the conversation is a referral to someone in your target market. It doesn't have to be someone who is ready to buy, and in fact, your contact will probably not have that information. Besides, you want to be known to your ideal prospects regardless of where they are in their buying cycle. In fact, if you can get to them early enough and start building a relationship, you might be the first and only person they'll call when they're ready to move forward.

But the mistake would be to go straight in and ask for the referral now by saying, "Can you give me names of people you think I should talk to?" The danger is that your contact may be unable to pluck a name out of thin air. The conversation will either grind to a halt or you'll get a couple of names that may not be on target. Therefore, what you want to do is help your contact filter a mental Rolodex to narrow in on the best one or two names to give you.

I find the best way to go through the filtering process is to do it together by asking questions. Productive interactions always have their basis in questions. "I was thinking the head of marketing would be a good person to talk to, or maybe someone who works in customer acquisition. Does that sound right to you? Or do you think starting somewhere else might be better?" By talking generally, rather than pressing for specific names, you've jump-started the filtering process and kept your contact actively engaged in the conversation, without adding any pressure.

4. Keep the Pressure Off No Matter What

Part of my success in networking has come from removing all pressure on my contacts when I interact with them. I know others are more aggressive, but that approach doesn't work *for* everybody or *on* everybody. I'm not a psychologist, but in my experience I've noticed that when the pressure is off, people are more relaxed, and the conversation flows more easily. They'll ask more questions, offer more advice, try to understand more fully what I'm doing, and in the process, will usually think of a way they can help. They'll offer their own call to action, one that's appropriate for them to give. You may actually get the lead you want, and perhaps even some additional help you wouldn't have thought to ask for, and your contacts will be more likely to follow through on their own ideas for helping you.

In contrast, when people are under pressure, they get tense. And when they get tense, their first instinct is to flee from the source of that tension. To be successful in networking, you want to make people feel comfortable and keep them *in* your network, not agitate them and push them away.

I'm usually able to get referrals and additional contacts without putting people on the spot. Through my line of questioning, they get a good sense of whom I'd like to meet, and before any prompting from me will often suggest a few people I should talk to. If not, I might summarize the conversation at the end of the meeting by saying, "So you think the division sales director would be the most receptive to my message? Well, if anyone you know comes to mind and you feel comfortable making an introduction, I'd appreciate it."

Accept that not everyone will be able to offer up a referral. Not because they don't want to, but perhaps because they don't have the right information or know the right people. Don't insist on getting a referral, though. Early in the formation of my business, I took a networking seminar where the instructor recommended that at the end of every meeting we ask for names and contact information of three more people to talk to. While that's not a bad idea on the face of it, the way he suggested asking was very off-putting. He directed us to say at each meeting, "Let's do this. I'll give you some time to look in your Rolodex for three more people you think I should meet, and I'll call you tomorrow to get those names. Okay?"

That felt uncomfortable to me. I imagined what it would feel like to be on the receiving end of that request, and I didn't like it. I'd rather get the name of the one referral people think of on their own, that really fits with what I'm trying to do, rather than three contacts they give me just to get themselves out of an uncomfortable phone call.

5. Wrap Up the Meeting

Keep your ears open throughout the conversation for opportunities to offer help. Along the way, your contact may mention certain information or a recommendation they need. If there's any way you can assist, now is the time to volunteer. If nothing came up, before you part ways, ask, "Is there anything I can do to help you right now?" Even if there is nothing your contact needs, the fact that you offered will build goodwill.

Thank your contacts for their time. It's my rule of thumb to foot the bill for the coffee or the lunch if I asked for the meeting, yet I find that most people will insist on splitting the check, which is also fine. Don't wait too long to send a thank you note. Preferably a handwritten one, if you can get it done quickly and in the mail within 24 hours. Otherwise, send an e-mail. If you promised to send any information, include it in your note, or mention you'll be sending it shortly. Your note will naturally prompt your contact to send any information that you were promised.

6. Keep Them Posted

Let your contacts know the results of any help you get from them, whether or not the opportunity panned out. Always be gracious. If a referral didn't work out, be appreciative and stay upbeat. You can say, "The company decided to go in a different direction, but I really enjoyed meeting Tom and wanted to thank you again for making the introduction." Reconnecting is not about getting hired or getting referrals right off the bat. It's about reestablishing the lines of communication so that you both feel comfortable reaching out to each other when the ideal opportunity arises and offering other forms of help in the meantime. Any immediate help that comes your way is pure icing on the cake.

NETWORKING SUCCESS STORY 5
REACHING INTO YOUR PAST TO SHAPE YOUR FUTURE
Tracey Segarra, Director of Marketing
Citrin Cooperman & Company
New York, New York

Four years ago, Tracey Segarra was a mother of three-year-old twins, working at a job she hated at a trade magazine for accountants. "I'd always been a natural networker, although I never thought that's what I was doing. So when I decided that I'd like to try to get into accounting marketing, I started calling the people I'd gotten to know over seven years writing about the industry."

A spokesperson at an organization who hated the critical articles Tracey wrote about it was one of the men who ended up helping her turn her life around. He helped Tracey polish her résumé and passed it along to a recruiter for a marketing director position that she was not qualified for. (Tracey had no marketing education or experience.) The recruiter wouldn't even pass her résumé along.

At the same time, another contact in the industry, whom she had taken out to lunch a few times to get to know his boss for a story, also heard about the same job. He recommended her to the firm's managing partner, and within a few weeks Tracey was hired.

"I'm now making more than double what I made as an editor, and I'm working for an entrepreneurial organization that isn't afraid to take risks (they hired me, didn't they?). And I have two people, who were peripheral to my job and really barely knew, to thank. Networking works."

CHAPTER 6

CULTIVATE NEW ALLIANCES
BUILDING BRIDGES TO NEW CONNECTIONS

> If a man does not make new acquaintances as he advances through life,
> he will soon find himself alone.
>
> —*Samuel Johnson*

The *New York Times* ran an article a few years back on networking burnout which profiled folks who'd been out of work for so long that networking was no longer an effective job-search tool for them. I know that networking works when done correctly, so I read the piece with great interest—and suspicion. As it turns out, the trouble wasn't with networking, but whom these job hunters were networking with. They returned over and over again to the same pool of friends, neighbors, and colleagues, eventually wearing out their welcome, until inevitably their contacts shut down and stopped taking their calls. In effect, the networks of these job seekers were actually shrinking!

While help will usually come more quickly from someone who already knows, likes, and trusts you, part of your career development or business-building efforts should always be focused on making new connections. You don't want to put all your eggs in a small basket of relationships. Continually extending your circle of contacts expands the help available to you from your network when you need it. And while it's never too late to start, it's never too early either.

Filling Up Your Dance Card at Events

Why did Willie Sutton, one of the FBI's 10 most wanted fugitives in the 1950s, rob banks? "Because that's where the money is," he said. Networking events are where the networkers are. If you want focused, concentrated time with people who are interested in making new connections, networking events should be a cornerstone of your strategy.

Events are also a great way to reconnect with people already in your network who don't see you that often. At a professional association cocktail reception, I ran into Frank, a man I knew from another networking group but hadn't seen in a while. He had just come from a meeting with one of his best clients, who needed a lot of help with his organization. Frank said he was thinking about connecting his client with Heather, an organizational development expert he found in the members' directory but had never met. When he saw me that evening, he asked me if I knew her, which I didn't, but as we talked more, Frank realized that his client should meet me as well to discuss developing an overall business strategy. He made the introduction for us later that week, and both Heather and I got the job.

Don't overlook the notion that business networking can happen almost anywhere people gather for business, whether it be a formal networking group or even a marketing seminar. Classes and seminars can be fantastic opportunities to learn something new that will boost your professional development and expand your professional contacts. While you're fueling your needs and interests, you're also meeting others with the same needs and interests, and opportunities to partner or help each other will be abundant.

Certainly you can also network in social settings, but my personal style is to keep the two separate. Could I make a connection or two standing in the buffet line at my cousin's wedding? Possibly, but I'd rather let that happen organically rather than aggressively working the room when everyone else is diving for the crab cakes.

Networking Unconventionally: Connecting at Conferences

I'm a huge fan of networking at conferences, which are just events on steroids. In one day at the right conference, I can get all my networking done for the year in terms of making new connections. I'll still need to follow up after the event in order to forge deeper business relationships, but I don't feel the pressure to go to events every month to keep replenishing my network with new contacts.

What I find appealing is not just the sheer number of attendees that conferences and industry trade shows attract, or the multiple ways to connect with people—at breakout sessions, during breaks, around the exhibit hall—but also the spirit of openness and collaboration that surrounds big events. Conference organizers tell me that the number-one reason people attend is to network. That means that people want to meet you. It's easy in these types of environments to approach people and introduce yourself. It's expected. And since not many people are good at this, if you take the initiative, you'll save them from feeling awkward and alone in a crowd, and they'll appreciate it.

How do you do it? Easy. Here's a sample of a typical exchange. I'll simply turn to the person sitting or standing next to me, extend my hand, and say:

ME: "Hi. I'm Liz Lynch."

ATTENDEE: "Oh, hi. Ann Nelson."

ME: "How are you enjoying the conference so far?"

That's all you need to do to get the conversation started.

The other great thing about conferences is that nearly everyone is accessible, even top-billed speakers. At one conference I attended last year, a woman I met who hosts a radio show in Texas saw former Hewlett-Packard CEO Carly Fiorina, who was scheduled to give the keynote, standing alone at the cocktail reception. She went over to introduce herself and spoke to Carly for nearly 20 minutes. She even got Carly's card and her agreement to appear as a guest on her show. Imagine trying to get a Fortune 500 CEO on the phone for 20 minutes by cold-calling her office. It wouldn't happen. But at a conference, people are much more approachable and, in fact, they expect to be approached (unless they're surrounded by the Secret Service, of course).

How to Find Events and Conferences

There are numerous sources you can turn to to find relevant events or conferences for your industry, profession, or region:

- Get recommendations from clients and colleagues.
- Look in your local business newspaper or publications for listings. For example, in New York, Chicago, and Detroit, *Crain's* lists a multitude of events for the coming week both in its magazine and on its Web sites.
- Use Google to search your topic of interest and add "conference" or "networking event" as additional terms in the search box.

- Search for areas of interest on Meetup.com, an online directory that allows you to find events by keyword or geography.
- Visit the Web sites of key industry associations to see when and where they're holding local meetings and national conferences.
- Check out Trade Show News Network (tsnn.com) and Trade Show Week (tradeshowweek.com) for listings of events by industry and region, including international shows.

For bonus articles on networking at conferences, visit www. smartnetworking.com.

Transcend Your Name Tag:
Raise Your Event Profile

If you do attend conferences and events, the best way to maximize your time is to do more than just attend.

To connect with others, you have to put yourself out there. But doing it the smart way focuses less on "working the room" and more on taking on roles that allow you to stand out from the rest of the crowd—and have the room come to you. If you're going to an event anyway, why not try to raise your profile? It may require you to arrive earlier and work a tad harder than you'd have to as an ordinary attendee, but the payoff will be exponentially higher. You'll end up meeting more people, more will seek you out, and event organizers will be grateful for the help.

The Buck Starts Here: Work the Registration Table

When I'm new to an organization, this is one of my favorite places to be because I can meet a large percentage of attendees. I can see who's coming, introduce myself, and place faces to names. Plus, it puts me in a great position to be a connector and make introductions between people who would benefit from getting to know each other.

Greet and Meet: Make First-Timers Feel Welcome

Volunteering to welcome attendees to an event gives you the perfect excuse to say hello to everyone who walks through the door. If you're at all shy about approaching people, but have the explicit job of greeting attendees or giving them directions on where to go next, you'll have less trouble starting conversations. It's almost as if the role itself gives you the courage and the purpose to approach others. Over time, approaching people will come more naturally to you.

Even if meeting people is already very comfortable for you, welcoming participants to a meeting has wonderful benefits. Michael DeCamillis of Dolvin Consulting in Trenton, New Jersey, is part of the ambassador program at his local Chamber of Commerce which strives to create a "welcome home" feeling at meetings by having existing members greet new people and those who look lost or alone. While this helps everyone feel more at ease and increases chamber membership, it also helps Michael reach his goal at every event of having a meaningful conversation with five people he's never met before.

Stage Presence: Introduce the Speaker or a Sponsor

In just a few minutes on stage, everyone in the room can know who you are and what you do. At one conference, I spoke at the morning break-out session and during the afternoon introduced the author and life coach Cheryl Richardson at another session. I was able to get in front of a whole new audience while introducing Cheryl, reaching twice as many people at the event than if I had limited myself to just my session.

Even the most reluctant public speakers find that giving a brief introduction is one speaking role they can handle. I should know. That's how I started. Early in my business I decided to launch a networking group for independent consultants in the New York City area so I could meet others who did what I did and start to build a referral network in case I needed help on larger projects. I also thought it would be a great way to meet prominent people in the business community and invite them to speak at our events. I asked my friend Lisa to chair the group with me, and we took turns opening the meeting and saying a few words to introduce our speaker.

Lisa was always a natural on stage, but I really had to work at it. When it was my turn that month, I would practice my intro for days. Days! For a 2-minute speech! Did my voice quiver with nervousness the first few times? Of course. But after a while, I felt comfortable enough in front of a crowd of 30 people for 2 minutes, that the idea of speaking for 10 minutes on a panel at other events and then giving my own 75-minute workshops on networking was a natural migration. Now I regularly speak to large audiences, and while I still feel a twinge of nervousness just before I go on stage, it always subsides once I get started. (Read Chapter 9 for more about speaking to attract people into your network.)

The Group Hug: Networking by Association

In 2003, I had the privilege of delivering a presentation to the New York chapter of the Association of Real Estate Women, a dynamic and diverse group involved in all aspects of real estate, including architecture, law, building security, and banking. During the session, several of the members shared powerful stories about networking within the group that led to incredible business opportunities.

Joining a group gives you a sense of belonging when you feel connected with others around a common interest. The more events you attend, the more you'll feel at home because your relationships deepen through shared experiences. You'll build a base of support with regular members and position yourself with new members and guests as someone in the know.

Organized groups also add structure and frequency to your networking which can be especially helpful for people starting to build their networks. Because groups tend to meet on a regular basis, and often on the same day and time each week or month, you can put those meetings into your calendar in advance. Blocking out networking time in your schedule means that you're more likely to do it. Groups can also be helpful for experienced connectors, particularly for those who do better with a more structured networking program than a self-directed one.

There are many different types of groups you can join, each with its own advantages and disadvantages, depending on your situation. Following are ones you're most likely to find in your area.

Industry Groups

Nearly every profession you can think of has an industry association that does one or more of the following (and then some): organizes an annual conference, researches trends, hosts educational programs, and advocates for the industry. If you're planning a career in a particular field or if your target customers belong to a specific group, join that association and become an industry insider. You'll keep up to date on important people, innovations, and news, and if you're able to attend the organization's biggest events, you'll raise your profile and become known, liked, and trusted by key players over time. The downside is that membership can sometimes cost several hundreds, or sometimes several thousands, of dollars. In addition, it can also be exclusive, meaning you have to be invited to join or have reached a certain level within your company.

General Networking Groups

These organizations tend to be focused more on a specific geography rather than a particular industry. Examples include the Chamber of Commerce and Rotary clubs, which attract people from all fields and are great for networking across professions. If you find yourself running into the same folks over and over in your industry association, general networking groups help you mix it up with a different crowd and build a whole new branch of your network. But because they do attract everybody, you have to do a little more work to figure out whom you should spend time networking with. One way to shortcut the process is to give a seminar or presentation in your area of expertise and see who approaches you.

Referral Groups

Members in groups such as LeTip and Business Networking International (BNI) meet weekly to exchange leads with other members. Typically, only one member per industry is allowed to join a group in order to prevent conflicts around which member to give a lead to. Therefore, within a city or region, several different chapters can coexist, and you need to find one with an opening in your profession. I joined one of these groups early in my networking career on the recommendation of my Web designer, who had also referred me to two other members in his group, a printer and a sales rep for a Web hosting company. Frankly, I found it a bit too intense for me that early in the morning, but I still keep in touch with several people I met there who still belong to the group and get great value from it. Each group has its own personality and mix of professions, so it's important to attend a few meetings as a guest, preferably of several different groups, before committing to one.

Peer Groups/Masterminds

In *Think and Grow Rich*, Napoleon Hill touts the benefits of master-mind groups as a critical step to riches. "A group of brains coordinated (or connected) in a spirit of harmony will provide more thought-energy than a single brain," he wrote. Peer groups and mastermind groups bring people together from different companies who are at similar levels to discuss their business growth issues and get advice from people in the same boat. Examples include Young Presidents Organization and Vistage, but there are plenty of private mastermind groups as well. Though they're not networking groups per se, members often build strong relationships there through the experience of learning about one another's businesses and experiences and getting valuable feedback and expertise on their challenges. The know, like, and trust factor among members is high, and they'll frequently turn to one another for new business opportunities and recommendations.

Alumni Groups

Many schools and some large companies have active alumni networks. Check their Web sites for online user groups and news about events and get-togethers. I belong to several e-mail groups for Stanford Business School, as well as a Yahoo! group for Booz & Company where members frequently post business opportunities as well as a list of upcoming events. They'll also sometimes pose questions or requests for referrals, which is a great way to raise your profile in the group and help a fellow member at the same time.

Browse LinkedIn and Facebook as well (more about this in Chapter 12), since more and more of these institutions are creating online groups at these sites. Although sometimes joining an alumni group at one of these social networking sites entitles you to little more than permission to include the group's badge on your profile page, as these sites evolve and groups get more savvy about using them, you'll be able to leverage the community more easily.

There are probably other groups in your community you might consider depending on your interests and passions. For example, lending your time to a nonprofit group whose cause matters to you allows you to meet prominent people with the same objectives. The same applies to a political organization. There are also professional groups that form locally around a very specific industry area in a region and may not have a national affiliation.

Many networking groups allow you to attend their meetings and events without becoming a member so long as you're willing to pay a higher registration fee. In fact, before you pay any fees to join a group, make sure you attend some of their events first as a guest or nonmember to see what the group is like and whom it attracts. While you're there, pick up their latest newsletter and talk to as many members as you can. Ask about their experience with the group, how long they've been involved, what they like about it, and what could be improved. Hopefully you'll get some candid answers that will help in making your decision to join.

Keep in mind that some companies may host internal groups for employees around approved topics or activities. For example, there may be book clubs, sports teams, or Toastmasters groups that meet regularly and attract a diverse cross section of employees. These groups help build camaraderie, and even if they aren't explicitly for networking, they'll force you to get out from behind your desk every once in a while to meet some new people.

Join only as many groups as you feel you have the capacity in your schedule to handle. Becoming deeply involved in one or two groups, especially the most important ones for your industry or profession, can often be more efficient (and fulfilling) than flitting around the surface of a handful.

How Do You Find Groups?

Groups abound in every major city, and most have regular events. You can search Google for a list of associations in your industry or check ads or listings in your local business newspaper. One of my favorite ways to find new groups is to ask others. Whenever I sit down for follow-up meetings with contacts, one of the questions I always ask is which groups they belong to. I'm always interested to know what's working for other people. Whenever I give seminars, I often pose the question to participants and list on a flip chart the groups that are mentioned. That way, everyone in the room has an initial prospect list of groups to investigate.

You can also ask peers, mentors, and colleagues in both your current field and target industries about the groups they belong to. We all like to share information, especially if we believe it could help someone. When you get recommendations, check out the Web sites of groups that sound intriguing. Ask your contacts about upcoming events their groups might be hosting. If any seem interesting, go. At least you'll know one other person there.

Asking clients and customers is also smart, especially if they're open to bringing you to a meeting as their guest. You'll meet their peers, who might also be good prospects for your business. And if you show up with your clients, they'll be able to introduce you around, effectively giving you their implicit endorsement. It's very important at these types of meetings not to be in sales mode. You want to respect the environment of the group and act like one of them. Focus on making the initial connections and follow up later.

Networking groups and professional organizations have helped me make sure I meet new people and get exposure to new ideas on a regular basis. But it can be hard to find just the right group, and sometimes you grow out of one. Don't be afraid to try out different groups and leave those that are no longer serving your needs. If you do, you don't have to leave those relationships behind. You can still stay in touch with those you have the strongest connections with.

NETWORKING SUCCESS STORY 7
FINDING YOUR HOME AND THE
INSPIRATION TO PURSUE YOUR DREAMS
Pam Narvaez, Small Business Consultant
Start-Up Specialists
Austin, Texas

Pam Narvaez volunteers for an organization called Girlstart and was a presenter at its big event last year, "Expanding Your Horizons." The room volunteer assigned to her was a woman named Misty Adair. They immediately hit it off and began chatting between sessions. During the lunch break, Pam suggested they exchange numbers so they could present together at the event next year.

"When she saw my business card, she immediately invited me to join her networking group "Business and Balance" headed by Renee Trudeau. I was shocked. I wanted to meet with Renee after seeing her present at an event the year prior, but I just didn't think I could afford her services. And now here I am being invited to join her free networking group!"

Pam joined and discovered a whole new world of women and instantly felt a deep connection with them. It turned out that Renee had just published a new book, *A Mother's Guide to Self Renewal*, and Misty was leading one of her personal renewal groups for mothers. So Pam joined Misty's group, meeting more amazing women, and the entire experience has changed her life completely. "I have the direction and deeper personal connections in my life to finally make the career change I have dreamed of—leave the corporate world and work as a professional consultant."

CHAPTER 7

MATTER TO THE PEOPLE WHO MATTER TO YOU

SEIZING OPPORTUNITIES TO CREATE VALUE AND HELP OTHERS SUCCEED

> Make yourself indispensable and you'll be moved up.
> Act as if you're indispensable and you'll be moved out.
>
> —*Anonymous*

Let's cut to the chase. At the end of the day, the main reason we network is to be in the flow of potential opportunities. Ideally, you want to be the first and preferably the *only* person called for a new job or business venture. The more you network, the more opportunities you'll see, but not every one of them will have needs that you can fulfill yourself. You have two choices: ignore the opportunity because it's not relevant to you specifically, or refer it to someone in your network who can take advantage of it.

By making the effort to make the referral, you create value for two people in your network—the one with the need and the one who fills it—and you gain as well. You reaffirm that you are valuable and relevant to your contacts. By choosing to pass, on the other hand, you force your contacts to look elsewhere for help, and the additional value that would have been generated in your network, now gets created in someone else's network.

We Have Unlimited Value to Offer If We Know Where to Look

Value is important in sustaining your network. It can help grease the wheels for following up with new connections and make it easier to stay plugged in with your relationships so that you stay top of mind. Value is created from the help you provide, which in turn increases the quality of life for those around you. They are better able to do their jobs, to make progress toward an important goal, and to help more people themselves.

Value can take on two different forms—either tangible or intangible—and each of us can find at least one way in one of those forms to be of service to those around us. Let's look at some of the options for tangible value first.

Tangible Value: Help People *Get* Something

Tangible value is created from the specific things you do that directly help people move toward an important objective. They can include:

- Connecting prospective buyers with sellers
- Making introductions to potential business partners
- Recommending a friend for a job
- Gathering information on a colleague's behalf
- Sharing your expertise to help someone make a decision
- Providing access to people, places, or experiences

If you can help solve a problem or create an opportunity someone wouldn't otherwise have, you've just generated tremendous tangible value within your network. Even if you don't have a huge contact list or the advantages that some of your competitors have, you can get creative and develop something unique to offer.

What's the unique tangible value you can provide to your network, or to those you want to attract into your network? What do you know more about than your colleagues or competitors? What special skills do you have that others can use? What organizations are you involved with that might benefit those around you?

College students and young professionals ask me all the time, "I'm just starting my career. What value can I add to someone I'd like to network with who has 30 years of experience on me? Surely there's nothing I could offer that they couldn't easily get elsewhere." Just because you're young doesn't mean you have no tangible value on your balance sheet. You just may not realize it yet. The knowledge you've acquired in your studies, specific expertise you've gained from a lifelong hobby, your involvement in clubs, and your relationships with classmates and faculty are all things you can tap into. Don't undervalue your technology talents either. A generation that grew up with instant messaging can be a great help to someone whose secretary still takes his messages. If you don't have these assets now, get them. Your network has no use for a bump on a log, and it's no fun helping one either.

Recently I spoke at a conference in Boston, and after my panel session, I presided over a booth in the exhibit hall which I had arranged with the conference organizers called the "Networking Coaching Corner." There, attendees could visit me throughout the day to get advice about networking and ask questions about their specific situation. I know that for many people conferences can be overwhelming, and although participants know they are there to network, they often don't know how.

One young lady approached me and thanked me for the tips I shared during my session. She mentioned that she was a junior at Harvard and involved with an organization that develops leadership programs for students, faculty, and officers of the college. She liked my clear approach to networking and asked if I would be interested in giving a presentation to the group's members. Though she's still in school, through her involvement in that organization, she's able to create value for the entire Harvard community, as well as for speakers, authors, and anyone with knowledge to share. That's a lot of value to a lot of people.

No matter where you are in your career, you can always find ways to add value. But you have to get out of your house or away from your desk and get out there. Look around your community, your school, or your company for organizations whose mission you have a passion for and get involved. Or find an activity you love and develop a skill. Whether you love helping disadvantaged kids or can set up a Facebook page in less than eight minutes, that passion or proficiency is value you can use to benefit your network.

Intangible Value: Help People *Feel* Something

Typically when we receive tangible value—a referral to a client, a recommendation for a job—we also get a heaping side order of intangible value.

We feel warm and fuzzy about who helped us, and we like them even more. But we can also get intangible value on its own. We can feel warm and fuzzy about people simply when they interact with us in a friendly and sincere way, even when they're not providing quantifiable help.

Tangible value is something we give outright. Intangible value is an outcome of how we interact with people. In *The Power of Charm*, Brian Tracy and Ron Arden outline five characteristics that help win people over: acceptance, appreciation, approval, admiration, and attention. These are often a by-product of authentic interactions we have and not things we should strive to deal out directly. We can't enter into a conversation thinking, "I'm going to shower this guy with admiration and see if I can get a few referrals out of it." That just doesn't work. What if those referrals never come? You'll feel impatient and angry, and the other person will feel used.

The test with all your networking interactions has to be, "Will you feel good about how you conducted yourself even if you get back nothing in return?" If you let go of your expectations for any outcome and just be friendly, sincere, and interested in learning about people, you'll automatically make them feel accepted and appreciated. In turn, they'll feel more positively about you and more willing to invest in a relationship.

Here are some ways to offer intangible value to your network:

- *Provide support.*   When it makes sense for you and your business, using the products and services of those in your network can go a long way. While becoming someone's customer also provides tangible benefits in the form of revenues, the intangible benefits can often be greater. A few years ago, I wanted to schedule a follow-up meeting with a man I had met briefly, who, at the time, was organizing a lot of events and building quite a sizable networking community in New York City. When we got together, he told me that he doesn't have nearly enough time to meet with everyone who asks, but he said, "Because you came to one of my events, you got my attention. How can I help?"
- *Express gratitude.*   Thanking those who help you not only makes them feel appreciated, but it can also create some positive, tangible outcomes. When I first started my business, I sent a small thank you gift to a former colleague who became a consulting client. When he called to thank me for the gift, he spontaneously came

up with the name of another consultant he thought I should meet and gave me his phone number. I made contact, and three months later this consultant built me into his proposal for a lucrative project for one of his major clients. I got a huge amount of mileage from that initial thank you.

In contrast, a few years ago another friend referred two consultants—me and one other—to a client in need of both of our services. The client hired both of us. And as a thank you, I sent my friend a three-month subscription to the *Italian Wine Club*. The other consultant never even acknowledged the referral, which ultimately turned into a big account for her. I'm not sure if it was lack of manners, forgetfulness, disorganization, or all of the above, but there's no excuse for it. Right or wrong, my friend harbored negative feelings toward her and is unlikely to refer another client to her again.

• *Interact regularly.*   The more often you see people, the more chances you have of reinforcing positive feelings they have about you, and vice versa. That's why joining a networking group or online community can be so helpful in building close relationships. Interacting with the same people over and over again leads to shared experiences and deeper connections.

A great example is one of my Facebook friends Walter Akana of Threshold Consulting in Atlanta. When I launched my weekly video tip series *Passport to Networking*, in which I film a brief networking lesson from a different location in the world and post it on my Facebook page, Walter would post an insightful comment about that week's video that would add another layer to the story. Not only have his comments enhanced the viewers' understanding of the lesson, but they've also helped spread the word about the videos themselves. Although Walter and I have yet to meet in person, these consistent and positive interactions have allowed us to build our relationship and contribute to each other's success.

Leading with Value in All Your Interactions

Value can be a strong lead-in for any kind of follow-up or outreach that you do with your network. As Winston Churchill once said, "You make a living by what you get, you make a life by what you give." Think of how you can add value to people's lives when you plan to interact with them and you'll always be welcome. Here are some ways to make that happen.

Use Value for First-Time Follow-Up

You make a great connection at a conference or networking event, but how comfortable are you reaching out to that person later? If you often struggle to come up with a good reason to call, consider what Sun Tzu said: "Every battle is won before it's ever fought." What you do *before* the follow-up will make the process easy or hard. Here's a method for successful follow-up that starts at your first interaction.

1. *Uncover value through conversation.*   At an event where you'll be mingling with lots of other participants, you have a limited amount of time for conversation with each one. Therefore, don't spend 10 minutes talking about the weather. A little small talk is okay at first to break the ice, but move quickly to topics that move the relationship forward. Asking a question about the conference is a great way to direct the conversation into something more meaningful. Two great examples are: "So, what brings you here?" Or, "What have you enjoyed about the conference so far?" Then you can move on to broader questions to learn more about the person's goals and professional interests.

2. *Set the mechanics in motion.*   Establish a reason during the conversation to follow up. It's always easier to make the follow-up call or send the follow-up e-mail if you know people are expecting it. So connect with something they said during your conversation that can be a logical lead-in to sending them helpful information, recommendations, or suggestions. Make sure the reason to follow up is a value for them, not something that benefits just you. In other words, unless they specifically asked for it, promising to e-mail your sales brochure or your résumé doesn't count.

   Get a business card so you have complete contact info. This is much better than jotting down just a name and e-mail address on a napkin because now you'll have several ways to reach that person—e-mail, phone, fax, and mail. Even if you never intend to send a fax, it's good to know that you have the option. Recently I spoke on a panel with Andrea Nierenberg, author of *Million Dollar Networking*, who advised asking, "What's your preferred method of follow-up?" I love this because it tells people that you think so highly of them that you're willing to play on their terms.

3. *Make sure you're remembered.*   Write notes on the back of *your* business card. You always hear the advice to write notes on the back of business cards you receive so that you can remember something about the people you talk to. But how about trying the idea in reverse? Writing some notes about who you are and what you will follow up about on the back of your card before you hand it to someone is a great way to stand out and be remembered.

It's best to follow up within two business days, before the event fades into memory and life's daily emergencies consume us. If you're at a conference that ends on a Thursday and you'll be traveling to get back home all day Friday, it's okay to wait until you return to the office on Monday to follow up. However, if you know you won't be in until later in the week, at least send a short e-mail within the two-day time period to say how much you enjoyed meeting and that you'll send the info you promised once you've completed your travels.

4. *Ask for the meeting.*   If it's geographically possible, the ideal follow-up is a face-to-face meeting where you both have more time to learn more about each other and explore ways you can both benefit from your relationship. However, there's a wrong way and a right way to ask for the meeting. The wrong way focuses on you. Saying something like, "I'd love to get together so I can tell you more about my services," is not a compelling enough reason for most people to take the time out of their busy day to meet you. That's an e-mail message or voice mail that will almost certainly be deleted.

Even if he needs what you have to offer, it's always better to position the meeting as a mutually beneficial event where you can both learn more about the other. And mentioning in your note or phone call that you may have a helpful recommendation or idea shows you were paying close attention during your first interaction and could help you get the meeting set up more quickly.

Let him pick a date, time, and place for the meeting that he prefers, whether it's his office or the coffee shop next door. I also like to keep it short. In fact, proposing a shorter amount of time, say 30 to 45 minutes, will make it easier for him to accept because he'll sense that you'll keep the meeting focused. Then, if the meeting is going well, you can always go longer, but at least you'll have gotten through the tough part of getting the meeting in the first place.

5. *Orchestrate a successful meeting.*   At the meeting, be sure to ask questions that allow you to get to know more about his work and his objectives. He may reveal a need that you can address, whether it's a helpful suggestion or an offer to connect him to someone in your network. Spend more time listening than talking. If you haven't uncovered a way to help by the end of the meeting, close by asking, "Is there anything I can help you with right now?" If there is, it always feels great to help someone right away. If there isn't, he will appreciate that you asked.

   You should also prepare an answer to the question, "What help can I give you?" Most people love to help, but don't ask for too much too soon. Even if you need something at this very moment, you might hold off asking for it until you've had more back-and-forth dialogue and built a deeper connection. It all depends on how big your "ask" is. If you're looking for the name of a good real estate agent, that's easy, but if you're looking for an introduction to their CEO or biggest customer, remember that they're putting their professional reputations at stake, which they might not feel comfortable doing at this stage of the relationship.

If you subscribe to the philosophy of networking smart rather than hard, then follow-up isn't a numbers game. You don't have to spend time meeting hundreds of new people every year hoping that a handful of them will convert into good contacts. By following these simple steps, you can turn just about any contact you make into a lasting connection.

Offer Value in Ongoing Outreach

My friend Pam told me about a marketing campaign she implemented for her business that wasn't aimed at new prospects but at people in her existing network. These included attorneys and other professionals with whom she had worked in the past. She sent them a letter with some new information about her company and followed up with a phone call. The response was overwhelmingly positive.

It's not unusual to do a direct mail campaign to new prospects, but I thought it was a smart idea to reach out to former referrers and lapsed alliance partners with the same kind of professional, deliberate approach. No need to explain her business (they already know what she does) or convince them to work with her (they already had). Sometimes colleagues need a tiny push to remember that you're out there.

How often do we forget to reach out to our colleagues, tap them on the shoulder, and check in? We're so busy jumping into new networking events hoping to find that person to open the magic pipeline to an endless stream of customers that we don't have time left to work the network we already have.

That's one of the reasons I do an e-mail newsletter (more in Chapter 11). I land in the mailboxes of my contacts on a regular basis to share helpful content. While a newsletter or direct mail campaign may be a bigger resource commitment than you might be willing to make at this point, here are some other ideas to help you reach out to your existing network:

- *Forward helpful information.*   My friend Rachel has a consistent habit of forwarding newsletters and event notices to people on her mailing list whom she feels would benefit from the information. Quite regularly, she'll get a thank you response, and from time to time, she'll get new business from a past client or referral partner who suddenly "remembered" he needs her. But be judicious about how often you forward e-mails, and think carefully about who should receive them. You want to be sure they're relevant for the recipients.
- *Make a date for coffee.*   A great way to get caught up in person with minimal time commitment is to invite someone for coffee. To save even more time with going back and forth to my office, I try to schedule these catch-up meetings back to back on a particular day. One time, I even brought coffee and cookies to a contact's office because she was even more pressed for time than I was and couldn't get outside that day.

- *Refer someone to them.* What better way to say, "I'm thinking of you" than to send someone a lead for new business or a new strategic partnership? Some people have different philosophies on this, and I tend to be conservative, making referrals only when I see a very strong connection between two parties, not just the hint of one. That way, I don't waste anyone's time. So when I tell people in my network that they should meet a particular person, they know that I've put some thought behind it, and it shows that I've really listened to what they need.

- *Launch a "help offered" campaign.* Every so often, I'll pick out 10 people in my contact list and write a short e-mail that says, "Haven't spoken in a while, and just wanted to say hello. As part of my business development efforts, I've been doing a lot of networking lately and have met a lot of great people. If there's anything you need at this moment, please let me know. I may be able to help. Hope you're doing well."

- *Invite them to an event.* When I ran the networking group for independent consultants, I often offered to put new contacts on the guest list for a particular event so they could attend for free. They appreciated the gesture and many of them came.

Add Value by Making Connections

Making referrals and recommendations on behalf of others is a critical activity in networking and probably something most of us don't do enough of because we're too busy with our own issues. But it's important to make the effort and bring people within your network closer together.

When you become known as a go-to person, everyone will want to ask for a recommendation or be recommended by you, and your circle of influence will grow. Give generously and don't keep score. You'll be more effective at building a solid network when you keep your intentions pure. Here are five ideas to consider:

- *Connect someone to a friend.* Do you have two colleagues who've never met yet seem to be on the same wavelength and would benefit from knowing each other? Make the call. Arrange for the three of you to have lunch or get together for coffee. No obligation, no pressure, just a chance to introduce them and chat about what they have in common.

- *Connect someone to a **vendor**.*   Working with a vendor who's done an excellent job? Make a referral. A few years ago, I changed business banks. My new banker was so attentive, and I loved having someone I could call directly if I needed anything, so I took a few of his cards and handed them out to every small business owner I knew.

- *Connect someone to a **customer**.*   Have you looked beyond your area of expertise to find out what else your customers might need to make their businesses more successful? Do it now. We can get so caught up in our own area of a project that we don't think beyond the visible boundary. But the more of a resource you can be to your customers and the more connections into their companies you forge, the more valuable you become to more people inside.

- *Connect someone to a **resource**.*   Using a service that has helped you tremendously? Spread the word. I love recommending books, Web sites, events, networking groups, and companies to those I know could use the information.

- *Connect someone to an **organization**.*   Involved in a networking group or nonprofit cause that you feel strongly about? Share it with somebody. At a recent talk I gave, one of the participants was a new entrepreneur who was six months into her business and looking to connect with other women business owners. I gave her the contact info for the National Association of Women Business Owners, where I had once served on the board of the New York City chapter, so she could attend the next meeting.

Good networkers are generous with sharing information, resources, and contacts because networking is not just about getting what you need; it's about helping others get what they need too. Edmée Schalkx, a leadership development trainer and coach in the Netherlands, is involved in the American Amsterdam Business Club (AABC) and helped set up a nonprofit organization called Nabuur. At the end of 2005, she introduced the founder of the AABC to the CEO of

Nabuur who was looking for ways to strengthen the organization's role in aiding community development. Edmée knew that the founder could contact former President Clinton on behalf of Nabuur, and a year later the nonprofit got him involved in its mission of helping local communities all over the world. "While I gained nothing directly," she says, "the communities I was hired to serve were able to gain some much-needed support."

Sometimes, however, help can come back to us in delightful and unexpected ways.

NETWORKING SUCCESS STORY 9
HELPING FRIENDS IN NEED AND GETTING
HELP IN RETURN
Jan Vermeiren, Managing Director
Step by Step Consulting
Rumst, Belgium

Jan Vermeiren went to college in Antwerp, Belgium, and was a member of the student union board with another student, Joris. The two were good friends, but their contact decreased when they started working. Once in a while they would hear from each other, and they followed each other's careers from a distance.

A year after Jan started his own company, Networking Coach, Joris contacted him looking for a career change. Since tapping into the power of networking is the best thing to do when looking for a new job, Jan invited him as his guest to one of his workshops, thinking this would be the best solution to help him. He didn't expect anything in return; he just wanted to help his friend.

After the workshop, Joris landed a job at Nike. His career at Nike boomed, and a few years later he became country manager in Belgium. Remembering the easy-to-implement strategies he learned in a single half-day workshop, he called Jan to do a full training course for his management team to increase its sales results.

"Thanks to Joris I also got the opportunity to work with a company I like very much, but was otherwise very difficult to get access to. And who knows where this might lead? The lesson I learned from this experience is, give without expecting anything in return and you will receive (spontaneously) opportunities you might never have dreamed of."

Keep using value to connect and reconnect, and you'll show your contacts that you take the responsibility of being part of their network seriously. Send information on areas that are important to them. Be open to providing more help if they ever ask. And the best thing you can do? Send them customers. Not tire kickers who will take up their time with informational sessions, but people who are ready to work with them. Devote some time to showing your contacts that you're there for them and that you value your relationship. Their next big opportunity could already be sitting in your Rolodex at this very moment.

CHAPTER 8

PERFECT THE ART OF THE ASK

GETTING HELP IS INEVITABLE WHEN YOU ASK IN THE RIGHT WAY

> Ask the gods nothing excessive.
> —*Aeschylus*

Knowing how to build your network is crucial, but knowing how to tap into your network for help is even more important. After all, if you can't get the help you need for yourself or for others from the people you know, where *will* you get it?

Asking for help effectively is one of the most essential networking skills to master. But it's a delicate balance. Do it wrong, and you can damage the relationship. Do it too often, and you may be silently black-listed. Do it infrequently, and you're not allowing the give and receive to flow through your networking ecosystem. When you feel that you are moving toward your goals, you have more to give back to others. When you feel stalled, it can be hard to think beyond how to get out of your situation. That's why the airlines advise you to put on your own oxygen mask first before helping your children with theirs. You're not going to give help effectively if you're gasping for air.

The Hidden Dangers in Asking

Conventional wisdom says to go ahead and ask whatever the situation. Ask and you shall receive. Ask because what's the worst that could happen? That someone will say no? In fact, that's *not* the worst that could happen. What's worse is potential damage to your relationship. I'm not saying don't ask for help. What I am saying is that you need to think about how to ask for help in a way that increases your chances of getting it.

If you're in a transactional mindset where you don't expect to see the person again, you might take more risks with your ask. But haggling over a trinket in a bazaar is one thing. There's little harm in asking for a price that might be insulting because if you don't get it, it's easy to walk away and never face that merchant again.

However, if the relationship means something to you and if you want to continue doing business together in the future, you ought to think carefully about what to ask for. Asking for something that can be easily fulfilled creates positive feelings and strengthens the relationship. Asking for something outrageous that doesn't materialize can cause negative feelings on both sides. You can create an uncomfortable and unnecessary tension in the relationship when you put your contacts in a position of saying no to you. If they can't face telling you no, they may end up avoiding you altogether to escape guilt and embarrassment. A no can actually hurt.

An acquaintance once suggested I meet with a woman he knew, whom I'll call Elaine, believing there could be some synergies between her technology consulting firm and my strategy consulting business. Eventually, we may have been able to figure out what those synergies were had it not been for Elaine's bold ask at our first meeting and my subsequent failure at handling it effectively.

When we met, we shared some details of the projects we were working on. I was two weeks into a project at a major media company where I was brought on board as a subcontractor to another consultant who had sold the work and built the client relationship from the ground up. Elaine said, "I'd love to meet the CEO. Do you think you could make an introduction?"

Here's what I should have said, "As we get further along into the project and I spend more time with the CEO, I'll find an appropriate way to bring you up in the conversation." Instead, being overly eager to help, I jumped in without laying the groundwork properly with the CEO or the consultant I was working with. Not only did I create tension on the project, but I also lost credibility with Elaine because I couldn't get her the meeting.

Analyzing the Ask from the Other Side

In theory asking should be easy. Just open your mouth and ask. Right? Yet, if it were that easy, why don't we get everything we ask for or give everything asked of us? While I don't want to overcomplicate the act of asking for help, and you're certainly free to ask for whatever you want from whomever you want, if you are interested in increasing your chances for success when you ask, then it may be helpful to understand the thought process behind fulfilling your request.

Put yourself for a moment in the shoes of the people whose help you are asking for. Mentally, and often subconsciously, they're weighing your request along two criteria: how easy is it to fulfill, and what's the value to me of fulfilling it? But remember: ease and value are in the eye of the givers, not the requesters. It's important to look closely at both of these dimensions from their perspective.

Ease of Fulfilling the Request

Each person in your network will have a different ability to contribute to your goals, so when they hear your request, they'll ask themselves two questions: *how much time will it take* and *do I have the capability to fulfill the request?*

"How much time will it take?"
Remember that people are busy. If you look at your own to-do list, are there tasks that roll over from week to week and a growing list of unfinished projects? If so, what's *your* capacity to take on an extra favor or two? Therefore, consider the time requirements for fulfilling your request:

- Is this just a quick phone call or a brief e-mail to get some information or make an introduction?
- Is it something that requires a higher level of commitment, like mentoring or advising over the long term?
- Is it something in between, like agreeing to meet for lunch or give a 30-minute informational interview?

The more time consuming your request, the stronger the relationship you should have with that person before you ask. It seems like common sense, but some people seem oblivious to boundaries. Or they just want to take shortcuts, which highlights to me that they're more interested in getting what they need rather than developing a long-term relationship with me.

"Do I have the capability to fulfill the request?"

Next, your contacts will have to consider whether they have the skills, knowledge, and relationships necessary to deliver what you're asking. Now this is where your perception and theirs might diverge. Inherent in your request are assumptions about what they're able to do, which may not sync with reality. You may assume it's a snap for your contact to stroll into his CFO's office and recommend you for a new job or assignment, but in fact your contact may not have the relationship with the CFO that you think he has. You've put him in a real bind with your request, yet he doesn't want to lose face with you.

You're always better off asking for something that's not at all a stretch but would still be helpful to your cause. Think in smaller steps and get creative. People will help because they want to be liked too. But make it easy and give them a chance to succeed in helping you. My experience with Elaine taught me a lot, and I'm smarter today than I was back then. While I take full responsibility for my actions, one way Elaine could have phrased her request more productively for both of us was to say, "When and if you ever feel comfortable making an introduction, I'd love to meet the CEO." The first part of the sentence immediately takes the heat off and increases the ease of delivering from a capability standpoint. Relationships are fragile by nature, particularly when they're new, and little things make a big difference. Always view your request from the other side. Don't overreach, and do what you can to ease any pressure.

Value of Fulfilling the Request

If ease is what your contacts feel they'll have to *put into* your request, then value is what they feel they'll *get out* of it. As much as we like to think that pure kindness drives people to help us, our contacts may make a subconscious value calculation too. The two value-related questions they might ask themselves are: *will it make me feel good to help* (what's the intangible value) and *will it further my own goals* (what's the tangible value)?

"Will it make me feel good to help?"

Many of us get pure joy from helping others, and that's all the value we need. A few years ago, a former coworker wanted to make a big shift in her career and go into teaching. She was applying to teachers' colleges and needed a recommendation from a work colleague. Although we hadn't worked together in nearly 10 years and I hadn't seen her in about half as long, when she e-mailed to ask for my help, I didn't hesitate. Agreeing to write her recommendations was purely a feel-good decision that didn't benefit me directly, but it made me feel great to do my part, especially when she told me later that she was accepted to every program she applied to.

"Will it further my own goals?"

If people already know, like, and trust you, they will generally be open to helping you with your request based on the criteria we've already discussed. They won't be thinking about the potential tangible benefits they might receive. The intangible "feel good" benefits will usually be enough.

However, if your request would be challenging to fulfill in terms of time or effort, then it might be best to ask someone who could get some tangible benefit in return. Think about whose goals intersect with yours. For example, if you need to round out your board of advisors, which could be a significant time commitment many would not be willing to make, the people most likely to accept are those who would see tangible value in it for themselves. Perhaps those interested in being able to network with other board members and key constituents or whose company would gain from being aligned with your company in that way. That tangible value will often make it easier to get past some difficult challenges.

Who, What, and How to Ask: The Importance of Subtlety

Whether you're looking for a job or want to land a big consulting contract, there's usually more than one route to get where you want to go.

Deciding whom to ask for help and exactly what help to ask for requires some thought. Let's look at the two main sources of potential assistance.

Going Straight to Decision Makers

If you already have a relationship with the decision maker for whatever it is you want, you can contact them directly. But do not, I repeat, do not ask for the job or the contract. If you're not the right person for it, you'll create an awkward situation which might hurt the relationship in the long term. Remember, you always want to be thinking beyond this ask, to the ones you might need later.

What you should ask for instead is advice. If you know there is a specific job opening or request for proposal for a specific project, set up a phone call or a brief meeting to ask questions about it. Mention that you saw the posting and wanted to get some insight as to where the organization is in the process and what it's looking for. Obviously the decision maker knows you want to be considered, but by keeping the conversation at a high level and not asking for the position directly, you keep the pressure off and the conversation going. If the decision maker feels you're a fit, she'll come to her own conclusion that you should apply. If not, neither of you will have to face that uncomfortable silence. It's a subtle nuance to ask for advice, but extremely effective.

You can even follow this same approach of asking for advice from decision makers you don't yet have a relationship with.

NETWORKING SUCCESS STORY 10
INITIATING RELATIONSHIPS WITH THE RIGHT ASK
Daniel Markovitz, President
TimeBack Management
Corte Madera, California

In 2005, Dan Markovitz started a corporate training company that applies lean manufacturing principles to improve performance. This unique approach made him realize that he needed to learn more about lean and see if his ideas and approach had value. To that end, he set up a Google alert for articles related to lean and office productivity.

One day his Google alert picked up an article from a newspaper in Cincinnati. As part of the article, the journalist had interviewed a process improvement manager at a large, multinational manufacturing firm. Dan called the newspaper, got help in tracking down the freelance journalist, and talked with him for a while. He also got the contact information for the process improvement manager, whom he called.

They spoke for about 15 minutes. Dan didn't ask for a meeting to pitch his services, only for feedback on his ideas and approach toward lean. And for the next 18 months Dan would send the manager e-mails whenever he published something that he wrote or read an article that he thought the manager would find interesting.

"One day, a year and a half later, he contacted me asking if I'd be willing to give a speech at his company. That one speech has now turned into three additional engagements (one of them international), and the manager has been a wonderful reference for me with other potential clients."

Seeking Help through Intermediaries

Even if you know the decision maker, it can often be useful to seek help from an intermediary first, even if just to gather background information. In the case where you don't have any relationship with the decision maker, then an intermediary can definitely help pave the way for you if you set things up correctly.

The first place to start is with people you are already close to. The stronger your relationship is with them, the more value they'll get from helping you and the more willing they will be to step up and assist you with something that might take some time. In fact, that's the best way to go; get them engaged a few steps earlier in the process and they'll often suggest the most appropriate ways they can help you.

A few years ago, my friend Karen was looking for a new job and asked me to lunch. She wanted my advice about a job posting she saw at the parent company of a client I was working with at the time. She showed me the job description and asked about my experience with the client and what I knew about the corporate division and its culture. Never once did she put my capabilities on the spot to ask if I could get her résumé to the hiring manager. In fact, I think it was "my idea" to find out who the hiring manager was and see where he was in the process. It was also "my idea" to ask Karen to send me her latest résumé, which I volunteered to walk down to the hiring manager directly. Of course, this was the outcome Karen was hoping for all along, and our conversation was clearly leading to that point, but she never pushed it there. In my enthusiasm to help, I brought up these different ways I could assist in the process, and I had a higher stake in seeing them all through.

There's nothing wrong with asking for something short of what you ideally want, especially if it can still be helpful in reaching your goal; for example, asking for recommendations or advice on next steps, rather than a straight introduction to the decision maker. It may not get you all the way to the end zone, but a few yards closer is still good progress, and better for the relationship long term. In fact, you may end up getting closer than you think. Like what happened with my friend Karen, your contacts may say, "Sure I can do this small favor for you, but I can also do these three other things," and they'll feel great that they could overdeliver on what you initially asked for.

Be sensitive, however, about asking for free advice from someone who makes a living giving advice, like an attorney or a consultant. It's not appropriate, for example, to ask a small business attorney to sit with you for two hours to get her detailed feedback on a contract you're about to sign. If she offers to do it, great, but don't ask. That's taking money out of her pocket, and you don't want to be a mooch.

Final Thoughts on the Ask: Give All That You Can

Through the experience of helping others, we can often grow closer to them. Don't be afraid to ask for help, but give your contacts a chance to be successful in helping you.

- *Give context.*   By sharing the big picture, you'll help people understand what you're trying to do, where you are now, and, without having to ask them directly, what help they might be able to provide.
- *Give them an out.*   This is an instant pressure release valve that helps make your request *their* choice to fulfill, not your demand. Say, "I'd love to interview your old colleague Ken for the market trends section of my business plan *if you think he'd be open to it.*"
- *Give them a break.*   If people don't come through for you, don't take it personally. You don't know what's going on in their lives,

and perhaps some of the assumptions you made about how easy your request would be to fulfill weren't accurate. If you have a strong network, you can always find another way to get what you're looking for.

- *Give credit for whatever help you do get.*   Always be generous about saying thank you and sharing your appreciation whenever someone helps you, even if it falls short of what you were hoping to get. If that's all they were able to give you, accept it graciously.
- *Give your help in return.*   Whenever I write a thank you note, the last thing I always say is, "If there's anything I can ever do to help you, please don't hesitate to reach out." That shows my contacts that I am willing to help them whenever they need it, keeping the giving and receiving flowing throughout my network.

It's wonderful when opportunities find you automatically, but when you do need to ask for help, make sure to ask in the right way. Put the well-being of your relationships in front of your own needs and not only will you move closer to your objectives, but you'll also ensure that more help will be there for you in the future.

PART III

CONNECTING ONE-TO-MANY

OPENING DOORS TO UNLIMITED OPPORTUNITIES

CHAPTER 9

HEAD FOR THE LIMELIGHT

RAISING YOUR PROFILE TO STAND OUT FROM THE CROWD

> If you don't get noticed, you don't have anything . . . but the art is in getting noticed naturally, without screaming or without tricks."
>
> —*Leo Burnett*

Now that you've learned the critical skills necessary to be an effective networker face-to-face, taking smart networking to the next level is about putting yourself in places and situations where large groups of people can find you, learn who you are and what you know, and decide for themselves whether to network with you. This saves you time in two ways: by allowing you to spread your message to groups of people rather than to one person at a time and by attracting people into your network who are already predisposed to networking with you. It's a more subtle, less aggressive form of networking that puts your time to the best use and helps increase the quality of your network.

One way to do this is by building visibility with your target market to put yourself top of mind, giving you an edge over anonymous competitors. But I'm not talking about raising awareness of you and your company through advertising and putting buy messages out there that interrupt people in your market when they're trying to do something else (think banner ads and commercials). It always goes back to adding value by creating opportunities for others and sharing content and ideas when people are ready to listen.

Speaking at an event, for example, allows you to showcase your expertise and build the kind of credibility that no 30-second TV spot could ever accomplish. Starting your own networking or industry group gets your name in circulation and increases your circle of influence as you help people who are relevant to your world connect with you, with one another, and with new ideas.

Be the Star of Your Own Group

Over the years, a number of people have asked my advice about starting their own networking groups, unsatisfied with the existing alternatives around them. Whether you want to focus on a narrower niche, meet at a different time of day, or just structure meetings in your own way, starting your own group can indeed help you expand your network in more relevant directions. It can also give you valuable exposure that can help identify bigger opportunities for you.

NETWORKING SUCCESS STORY 11
SETTING THE STAGE FOR OPPORTUNITIES TO PROSPER
Bill Sobel, Chief Connections Officer
SobelMedia
New York, New York

In June 2006, at the urging of a media friend in Los Angeles, Bill started the New York: Media, Information and Exchange Group (NY:MIEG), drawing media professionals to monthly breakfast meetings that include lots of free-form networking time and a chance to hear insights from key innovators and top names in the industry. In Bill's words: "NY:MIEG is a place for executives in media, entertainment, and technology to meet with peers, share ideas, and develop friendships with the goal of assisting each other in reaching the next level or their personal goals."

Fast Company magazine called him a master connector. His mind is always racing about who needs to meet whom. NY:MIEG gives Bill a venue to make those connections happen on a much bigger scale. If you're interested in networking with people in broadband video or mobile media for example, just come to one of his events featuring that topic and you'll meet dozens of them.

In the process of building NY:MIEG, Bill has also built his own reputation and visibility. He's been contacted by companies all over the world who've heard of his events, read his blog, which is updated daily to keep NY:MIEG's message alive, and are primed to do business with him before even meeting him.

Bill has benefited tremendously from being the star of his own networking group. But it couldn't happen unless he was also creating value and opportunities for many others.

If starting an entire networking organization sounds like more than you can handle, you can still find ways to raise your profile in your community or company and bring together groups of people with a common interest.

A college friend of mine, Bret Allan, started a couple of lunch groups at work with people he shares something in common with: (1) coworkers who got their MBA at the University of Chicago (which apparently in Dallas is a rare group) and (2) coworkers who grew up in Los Angeles where Bret is originally from.

He says, "This provides a common link to initiate the contact and bring us together. Once we get to know each other, it is easier to keep the lunches going. We try to meet roughly once a quarter and pick a place within walking distance to the office to keep it casual. I have found that three to five in a group seems to be the optimal number—more than that is hard to schedule and loses the intimacy of the interactions. It has been an effective and relatively painless way for me to meet people in other parts of our large company that I might not normally interact with, and through the periodic contact of the lunches, keep up to date on what is happening in their area."

Don't Follow When You Can Lead

Taking on a leadership role in a networking group or organization that you would be involved with anyway maximizes your membership by giving you greater visibility and exposure than what would be available to the average member. As part of the leadership team, you might be highlighted on the group's Web site or in newsletters or events, for example, promoting you and your company to the rest of the organization as well as to the business community on a frequent and consistent basis. You'll attract people into your network who get to know you, and based on your involvement will begin to like and trust you too.

Leading always requires a greater time commitment than just showing up, of course, but depending on the group and the role, the payoff in higher visibility, greater name recognition, and increased connections for you could more than offset it. Plus, you'll be contributing something valuable to a group that is meaningful to you. Here are a few ideas for getting involved.

Join a Committee

For the highest visibility, I recommend joining the program committee of an organization. Typically the program committee never has enough manpower to execute all of the events the organization wants it to do. This committee will give you exposure at the event, as well as with potential speakers. It will also give you an opportunity to offer value to those in your network, and to those you'd like to attract to your network.

For example, when I ran my independent consultant's group a few years ago, a big part of every meeting was a presentation by a guest speaker. I used my position as the coleader of the group to contact local business leaders, entrepreneurs, and experts to invite them to speak at our events. Every single person was responsive to my phone call or e-mail, and while I felt they were doing me a favor by speaking at my event, I was also helping them get exposure to our members and sell more of their books, products, and services.

If programs aren't your thing, other committees may give you exposure to valuable groups in different ways. For example, working with the fund-raising committee may put you in touch with executives of locally based Fortune 500 corporations. Joining an advocacy committee may connect you with local politicians. You'll have to assess who the best audience is for your business, but don't forget to consider your strengths and passions as well. If you hate asking people for money, then fund-raising may not be the right place for you.

Run for a Board Position

If you're willing to commit to a higher level of involvement in an organization, whether it's a nonprofit association or a charity, joining the board of directors gives you significant exposure to influencers, both on the board and within the community. Board positions are not easy to come by, however. Often they are elected positions, so you'll have to gain support of enough people in the organization to win enough votes.

Make sure that you have a genuine interest in the mission of the organization. Being a board member often comes with a great deal of responsibility and time commitment. There are regular meetings to attend, and you may be asked to participate on subcommittees or task forces, so you don't want to do this unless your heart is in it. While you will obviously make great connections during your tenure, you don't want that to be seen as the sole focus of your involvement. You'll lose credibility if people see you spending all of your time networking and not getting your hands dirty with the real work of the organization.

NETWORKING SUCCESS STORY 12
SHARING THE BENEFITS OF AN INFLUENTIAL POSITION
Beth Polish, The Critical Junctures Group,
author of the DROOM® (Don't Run Out of Money)
Multimedia Series
New York, New York

Unexpected examples of positive networking karma have been part of Beth Polish's life ever since she started out in business. Recently, she experienced a chain of interlocked connections that led her to places she would not have gone otherwise, and ended up with an unforeseen opportunity to give back.

Beth serves on the board of the Women's Leadership Exchange (WLE), a company dedicated to supporting women business leaders, where she's also a growth guru traveling to the organization's conferences around the United States speaking on entrepreneurship, strategy, and finance. A fellow WLE board member asked her to join the board of ThinkQuest NYC, a nonprofit that helps inner-city students realize their potential by sponsoring fun, educational contests focusing on technology. As a former New York City public school kid who loves technology, Beth leapt at the opportunity.

One of TQNYC's largest sponsors is Best Buy. At a TQNYC meeting Beth got to talking with David Ring, the organization's champion at Best

Buy, and he told her that Best Buy is not only focused on giving back to the community (a major reason for their sponsorship of TQNYC) but also on supporting opportunities for women (both as Best Buy customers and as its employees). Beth let him know about the work she does with lots of women entrepreneurs and about her experience with the WLE.

"Finding my experience interesting, he introduced me to Julie Gilbert, the amazing woman behind Best Buy's innovative women's initiatives, and she hired me to give speeches to 1,000 of their women employees at their annual conference (a major business opportunity for me). And now it's all come full circle as I've been able to introduce Julie and Best Buy to the WLE, which is a great match for both organizations."

Volunteer for a Major Initiative

Whether you help organize the group's key fund-raiser or annual conference or make phone calls for its membership drive, contributing your time to a major initiative can give you exposure across the whole organization in a short amount of time, rather than committing to ongoing responsibilities.

Become Known through Public Speaking

Speaking at events gives you a public platform for your expertise. People interested in your topic will come to hear you speak because they'll want to learn from what you have to say. In one speaking slot you can get your message out to everyone in the audience, which takes a lot less time than meeting everyone in the room one by one.

Then, if and when they're ready to buy the types of products or services that you offer, you're likely to be top of mind. And, in contrast to a marketing brochure that someone might flip through or a Web site that someone might click through, a speech holds attention for a much longer period of time. By the end, the audience will feel they know you better, and perhaps like and trust you more as well.

Be careful, though. To be effective with this strategy, you have to be heavy on the content and light on the sales pitch. Rather than focus on telling how great your company is, give the audience members information that helps them solve a problem. Again, it always comes back to providing value. The irony is that by sharing content, you're marketing yourself more effectively than you would through a sales pitch.

Sometimes, you can get a lot of mileage from just the marketing of the event itself. For several years in a row, I worked with a company that organized a series of state conferences for women. Laurie, one of their managing directors, contacted me after seeing my name in an ad in the *New York Times*. I had been invited to speak at an event the newspaper was cohosting with Starbucks, and to promote it, they ran a full-page ad in the Sunday business section.

Laurie searched for me on Google, found my contact information, and invited me to speak on a number of panels and facilitate networking activities at several conferences attracting nearly 20,000 participants in total. This exposure led to other speaking engagements from corporate executives attending the conference who realized that their employees could benefit greatly from understanding how to network more effectively both inside and outside the company.

Speaking is an effective promotional and networking tool even if you're not a professional speaker. You can get valuable exposure for your company no matter what business you're in. Go to any industry conference, for example, and most of the speakers you'll see are practitioners in the field working anywhere from research to sales to business development to human resources. Here are some different options to consider.

Going Solo

This requires the most work for you because you're the only one on stage, but you also have more control over the agenda for the session as well as more time to share your expertise. You need to be comfortable speaking for a length of time, but that comes with practice. While carrying the whole show is often ideal, there are some easier alternatives that still get you up front without all the up-front work.

Hosting and Moderating

Your job would be to open the session, introduce the panelists, ask them questions, and take questions from the audience. It's more responsibility during the event than being a panelist, because you're controlling the flow of the session, but less work than carrying the whole program yourself.

Joining a Panel

Sharing the stage with other panelists is a good way to get started with speaking. That's how I began. Typically, panels are set up for each person to have five to ten minutes to speak and then answer questions posed by the moderator or asked by the audience. It takes less preparation than developing an hour or more of content on your own. The other nice thing about participating on a panel is the opportunity to build relationships with the other panelists and the moderator.

Leading an Interview

Interviewing is often harder than it looks. While it usually won't give you as much opportunity to share your specific expertise without seeming to compete with your guest, it can still be an effective way to get known. Just look at Oprah.

Speaking Virtually

Both old and new technologies are making it easier to reach audiences with your content without ever leaving your office. Three options include:

- *Teleseminars.* This is a live conference call where a speaker can give a presentation completely over the telephone to participants who dial in to a specific telephone number at a specific day and time. The bridge line technology helps manage the call so the speaker can mute out participants and their barking dogs while in presentation mode, and then open up the call for interaction in question-and-answer mode. The call can also be recorded and turned into a podcast.
- *Podcasts.* Think of this as a replay of a radio show that you're able to find online and listen to on your computer or download as an mp3 file to a player. Podcasting technologies allow speakers to record their content, distribute it through services like iTunes, and make it available for later listening.

- *Webinars.*   This is a presentation given over the Internet while participants sit in front of their computers to watch and listen. These are best when the presentation involves a product demonstration that would be hard to follow without the visuals. Again, these seminars can be recorded and accessed later, allowing you to share your expertise once and generate interest for your services over and over.

While the step-by-step methodology for creating your own virtual presentations are beyond the scope of this book, you can find a list of resources to help with both live and virtual speaking at www.smartnetworking.com.

If you can't stand the thought of speaking in public, you could appoint someone else in your company to act as spokesperson, attracting new prospects, business partners, employees, and investors for your business every time he or she presents.

Finding Opportunities to Speak

While you may not get paid to speak at events, it may still be an attractive opportunity if you're able to market your knowledge and expertise to a targeted audience. What you might miss in speaking fees you could gain many times over in client engagements or more customers. Here are some easy ways to find opportunities.

- *Through your network.*   Many of the folks in your network participate in organizations that run programs that need speakers. Let them know that you are using speaking as a marketing and networking tool and that you would love to deliver a program to their members.
- *Through your own research and outreach.*   Here in New York City there are many organizations putting on programs every week, and they all need speakers. Your local market probably has its share as well. Find local organizations that attract your target audience, visit their Web sites to get contact information, and call or e-mail to introduce yourself. Tell them who you are and what your expertise is. Mention that if they need a speaker for an upcoming event, you would welcome an opportunity to put something together to meet their members' needs.

- *Through other speakers.*   Speakers recommend each other all the time to organizations. For example, Allison Hemming, head of recruiting agency The Hired Guns, recommended me to an organization called the Freelancers Union, which serves the needs of independent workers. My networking seminar went very well, and I was asked to give one on business planning, which was a fit for my consulting company. While I could have easily developed a seminar on that topic, I felt that another friend of mine, Beth Polish, would be a better fit since she has taught that program for different organizations and already had materials prepared. Both of us have been invited back repeatedly to give more presentations.

  As a networker, recommending speakers for programs is good for me, because I can connect an organization that has a need with someone who can fill that need. And I have no problem recommending speakers in my field of expertise. There are times when I can't accept an assignment because of a scheduling conflict, and I'd rather recommend someone than leave the organization high and dry. Conversely, other networking experts have recommended me for opportunities that they weren't able to accept. So it's a two-way street.

- *Through word of mouth.*   I've found that speaking generates more opportunities to speak and have gotten a large percentage of my speaking engagements through word of mouth. For example, I'll speak for a local chapter of an organization and then get recommended to another chapter or for their national conference. Or people in the audience belong to other organizations and want to bring me in to do similar programs for their groups. In fact, I was recommended as a speaker for the Starbucks/*New York Times* event I mentioned earlier by a woman who had heard me speak at another event two years before.

A Word about Media and Publicity

There's nothing like a full write-up in the *Wall Street Journal* or *Inc.* magazine to help rev up your networking, but that kind of media coverage can be hard to get. Additionally, you'll have no control over what the story will cover or what pertinent information about you will be included. If a reporter interviews you, your words can be paraphrased, or the half-hour's worth of knowledge you shared might be condensed into one line.

Being a guest on a television or radio program can give you a little more control over your message, but there are challenges to getting booked in the first place, as well as time constraints for the segment. Still, being featured on a show or quoted as a source by a credible publication, particularly a national one, can definitely help you get known. Don't turn it away if you can get it, but don't pin all your hopes on it either.

CHAPTER 10

BLOG FOR BUSINESS
CONVERSING AROUND CONTENT
AND SHOWCASING YOUR EXPERTISE

If you can talk brilliantly about a problem, it can create the consoling
illusion that it has been mastered.

—Stanley Kubrick

Connections in networking happen through conversation. If you and I
meet at an event and start a conversation, we start to build a connection. The more we talk, the more we learn about each other, and the
deeper a connection we build. If, during our conversation I tell you
about my colleague Mary and that you two should meet, I've just started
to build a connection between the two of you.

Blogs follow a similar dynamic. Blogs house online conversations we
have with the world on the Web. When I post a link to an online article, I'm connecting my readers with that writer and her ideas. When
another blog links to a post on mine, that blogger is connecting me with
his audience. When my blog readers comment on a posting and I
respond, we're connecting with each other.

As Robert Scoble and Shel Israel say in *Naked Conversations*, blogs
are "word of mouth on steroids" because they enable conversations so
easily. Open your blogging software, copy and paste the link to an article or a blog post you've just read, type in some commentary about it,

click on "publish," and voila, within minutes you've just added to the conversation and initiated a connection with a worldwide audience.

Why Blog?

Webster's New Millennium Dictionary defines a Weblog, or blog for short, as "a personal Web site that provides updated headlines and news articles of other sites that are of interest to the user, also may include journal entries, commentaries and recommendations compiled by the user." In other words, a blog is your own journal where you can write about whatever you want.

When blogs first made their appearance, most of us didn't get it. I know I didn't. It seemed like people used them as online diaries, posting entries about the mundane details of their personal lives, like what they had for breakfast, who made them mad last week, and what they thought about the latest celebrity scandal. What was the point? Thankfully, the business world caught on to blogs as a powerful and easy-to-use publishing tool that enables anyone with a computer and an Internet connection to put ideas out into the world and to start and contribute to conversations.

As of August 2008, Technorati, a blog search engine, is tracking over 112 million blogs and estimates that 175,000 new ones are launched every day. While many of these are personal blogs, a growing number are run by businesses to market themselves. Why is this important to you? If your competitors are getting their ideas out into the world through their blogs and establishing themselves as experts in your industry and attracting opportunities, wouldn't you want to at least level the playing field by publishing your own blog?

Blogs Allow You to Share
Your Expertise with the World 24/7

Writing an article for a magazine or an online publication is a great credibility-building tool, but it's not that easy to get your article accepted, plus there can be a long lead time between article submission and publication. In contrast, you can post an article to your own blog in minutes, and you can post as often as you can think of new things to write about. Your blog is available online 24/7, allowing anyone with an

Internet connection to check out your expertise and network with you at any time from anywhere.

Blogs Build Intimacy with Your Audience

People can get to know you through your blog before they meet you. By reading through your current and archived posts, they can see the depth and breadth of your expertise and how you approach your topic. They can also get a sense of your personality. Intimacy builds trust. I've booked speaking engagements with organizations that have never heard me speak, but they have read my blog articles and connected with my approach to networking.

Blogs Are Loved by Search Engines as well as by Other Bloggers

Generally speaking, search engines favor sites that are frequently updated. Since blog software makes adding new content much easier than adding new content to your Web site page, your blog is more likely to be refreshed more often and, therefore, get ranked higher. In addition, blogging is very much a community, and bloggers like to network with and promote other bloggers.

Blogs Differentiate the Players in a Field

Let's face it. Don't most corporate Web sites sound alike? But visit corporate blogs, scroll through the posts, and the differences become more apparent. You can get an immediate sense of the depth of knowledge and the biases and filters each blogger brings to the subject: Who's writing? What are they writing about? What's their spin on the subject? How often do they write? What are they linking to?

Yes, You Need a Blog Even If You Have a Web Site

Harnessing the power of blogs in creating and expanding conversations will accelerate your networking by expanding your know, like, and trust factor with a large potential audience more effectively than your Web site can. Here are some key benefits to supplementing your traditional Web site with a blog.

Blogs Are More Engaging Than Web Sites

A Web site is more of a commercial vehicle than a blog is; it's a place the world can go to learn more about your products and services. On the other hand, a blog is more of a conversational vehicle. It encourages dialogue with your audience by allowing readers to share what they think about your topic and leave comments on your blog posts. Most Web sites don't allow for that kind of two-way dialogue. Also, there's more leeway on a blog to write in a more conversational and inviting tone, as if you were speaking with a friend, thus making your content more interesting to your readers.

Blogs Are Easier to Update

Blog applications have become so user-friendly that, if you can format a document in Word and send an e-mail, you can post to your blog. Setting up your blog initially will take some time, though it will be much faster than creating a Web site from scratch and you don't need any technical expertise. The application providers like WordPress, Type-Pad, and Blogger make it very easy. And because you're adding new content often, people are likely to visit your blog more frequently than they will your Web site.

Blogs Show Your Personality

Traditionally, Web sites are written like marketing pieces. That's what we're all used to seeing. There is certain information we expect to find—a products/services page, a client list page, a media page, and so on. On the other hand, we expect blogs to be more opinionated. The most interesting blogs are written for the reader, giving deep insight on a topic and covering many different aspects. Sometimes posts are humorous. Sometimes they're harsh. Sometimes they're controversial. By showing your personality, readers will see you as a real person and feel a greater connection with you than they would with a faceless corporate entity.

Blogs Show Your Authority

On your Web site, you want to keep visitors in, not push them out to other sites. However, blogs are different because readers expect you to bring the relevant parts of the Web to them. They're relying on your expertise to point them to other places on the Web that they should know about—to articles, press releases, Web sites and other blogs. In other words, while your Web site is all about you, your blog is all about the readers and the value you can bring to increasing their understanding of the topic. Ironically, that's precisely why your blog can display your authority more credibly than your Web site can.

Blog Basics

If you don't yet have a blog, here are some of the common questions you may have about starting one.

How Do I Set Up a Blog?

Do some research on other blogs to see what you like with respect to names, layout and design, writing style, and content. Use Technorati or a general search engine like Google to search for blogs in your area of expertise as well as blogs of your favorite authors and writers. Get familiar with their style of writing, what they write about, how they link to other content, and what else they include in their posts.

Then select a software platform, either a free one like Blogger or WordPress, or a paid service like TypePad, which charges a nominal fee for extra features and customization capabilities. It comes down to personal choice. You can see which platforms your favorite bloggers are using by looking on the side panels of their blog or at the bottom of the page. Each service will walk you through the setup process, which they've tried to make as easy as possible. Hey, if 112 million other people can do it, so can you!

What Should I Write About?

Because you'll be writing a lot over time, you definitely should write about something you know and enjoy. Ideally, it should be related to your business or area of expertise, but if you have a passion for fly fishing or photography, there's nothing wrong with starting a blog about that. It could certainly enhance your networking to share this personal interest, but just in a different way than if you focused on a business topic. While a business-related blog would show readers how you think about your subject, an interest-driven blog would let them learn more about you as a person.

Even better, find a way to combine the two to give your blog a very unique angle. You can use fishing analogies in your posts to explain certain concepts of personal finance, or photography metaphors to talk about leadership. My *Passport to Networking* video series, which I often refer to as my video blog, combines my twin passions of travel and helping people learn to network more effectively. I've talked about tearing down walls in your relationships from on top of the Great Wall of China, and the importance of being as consistent and reliable as London's Big Ben, with the famed tower chiming in the background.

Tone is important too. You'll notice in your research that the best blogs have a personality. They feel like they're written by a person, not a marketing department. People want to hear your opinion. That's what will make your blog content stand out and engage them. When you write your blog, think of yourself as a columnist rather than a reporter, and give your perspective on a situation, not just the facts. Add cleverness and wit—in your headlines, in your post topics, in your images—to keep readers engaged. Open yourself up, put your point of view on display, and let people know who you are. This builds your know, like, and trust factor more effectively than any marketing brochure ever could.

What If I Can't Write?

You actually don't have to write much. Blog entries aren't like magazine articles, which need a beginning, middle, and end. They're much shorter. If you're really hard-pressed, you can dictate your blog entry and have someone transcribe it. Or assign blog duties to one or more people in your company or to a freelance writer. It's important that whoever does the writing strives to create a unique voice because that's what will keep readers coming back.

How Often Should I Post?

Setting up a blog is the easy part. The bigger challenge is refreshing it with new content on a continuing basis. Some experts say that having a stale blog where the latest entry was posted six months ago is worse than having no blog at all. I'm not sure I agree completely with that. While you're not taking full advantage of all that a blog can offer, it's still beneficial to have an online archive of your content that showcases your expertise.

I've heard a range of opinion on how often you should post. Some say you should post several times a day to keep your blog fresh and the search engine spiders coming back often. Tim Ferriss, author of the *The 4-Hour Workweek*, said in an interview that he tends to post less often, maybe once or twice a week, because more frequent posting pushes the entries down the page before visitors can read them.

You also have to balance how you spend your time. The whole point of smart networking is to maximize results and minimize effort. If you enjoy writing, working on your blog and posting often may be a better way to spend your time than going to yet another mixer. On the other hand, if you struggle with writing, you may want to spend a minimum amount of time with your blog and focus on other networking activities. Strive for at least one posting a month to let visitors know that your blog is still active. Personally, I found that posting weekly was easier than posting monthly not only because my mind was always on the lookout for topics to write about, but also because it got easier to write the more often I did it.

Can I Blog as a Company Employee?

Since blogging about your industry helps develop your personal brand, it would be tempting to start a blog to build name recognition for yourself in your area of expertise, even if you work for someone else. But you should definitely check with your company on proper guidelines first, and even if there are no explicit rules, always be careful not to reveal insider information. To be safe, stick to commenting about and linking to public sources. If you know your stuff, you'll still have plenty to say. As an alternative, you can start a personal blog focused on one of your nonwork passions to make connections and build camaraderie with those who share that common interest.

Leveraging Your Blog for Networking

Once you've set up your blog, how do you best leverage it in your net-working, because that's the whole point here, isn't it? To become known, liked, and trusted virtually? Not just to blog for blogging's sake? The best approach is to think of your blog as both a one-stop shop where visitors can see the depth and breadth of your content expertise in action and as a tool through which you can connect with other blog-gers and the rest of the Web community who can spread your knowl-edge and credibility to their audiences.

Use your blog to develop a following. Here's what you can do to be found and to present a compelling case once you are:

1. Write a Strong "About Me" Page

I always get suspicious when a blog has no information about the author. If you want to create trust and gain credibility from your visitors, fill out the About Me page of your blog. You can copy the bio from your Web site or write something completely new. Be sure to include a link to your Web site for cross-marketing purposes, and upload a photo of yourself to help personalize your blog and give it a human face.

2. Announce Your Blog

Write your first few posts, the first of which should reveal your vision for your blog, what inspired you to start it, and what you plan to cover. This post will help welcome your readers and show them immediately what your blog is all about. Then, send an e-mail to your contacts let-ting them know you've launched a blog and invite them to submit com-ments. This starts the interaction with your readers that is so important in blogging and networking. Also, cross-promote your blog to make sure people can get to it from multiple areas. Create a link to it from your Web site, e-mail signature file, e-zine, and social networking profiles.

3. Add Feeds

If you want to develop a following, you need a way for readers to fol-low you easily and stay connected to your blog without having to visit it every day to check for new posts. RSS (Really Simple Syndication) is a way to deliver constantly changing Web content to feed aggregators like NewsGator, Yahoo!, AOL, and Google. Blog visitors subscribe to your feed, and headlines are sent via RSS technology to feed readers. They can quickly skim the latest headlines, click on any that catch their attention, and arrive at your blog to read your entries.

Some services like FeedBlitz also give subscribers the option to receive feeds via e-mail. Your post, or an excerpt of it, will be inserted into an e-mail message and sent to subscribers automatically. It's important to offer a variety of feeds to let your readers decide how best to follow your blog. If it's easy for them, it'll be easy for you. This is your automatic networking in action.

4. Network with Other Bloggers

Identify influential bloggers in your industry and begin networking with them by linking to their posts and leaving comments on their blogs directly. Use your full name in your comments so you can begin to build name recognition with the authors and their readers, and if you have the option to hyperlink your name back to your blog, do it.

And very important: make sure your comments add something to the conversation and give people a reason to click on your link and find out more about you. Don't just write, "Great post. Thanks." Finally, add a list of blogs you like to your blogroll, which is a set of outbound links to your favorite blogs usually listed on one of the side panels. You just might get added to their blogrolls too.

NETWORKING SUCCESS STORY 13
BUILDING VALUABLE,
VIRTUAL RELATIONSHIPS THROUGH BLOGGING
Pamela Slim, Writer and Coach
Escape from Cubicle Nation
Mesa, Arizona

Before Pam Slim started Escape from Cubicle Nation in October of 2005, she had no idea what a blog was. For the first three months, she wrote for an audience of four: her father and sister and best friends John and Desiree. Though they told her that they really enjoyed the posts, she realized that they were not exactly an unbiased sampling of her target market. So Pam just continued to write as well as read lots of other blogs in her areas of interest.

"My readership increased very slowly, from 4 to 20 to maybe 100 people each day." Then, late one evening in May 2006, she made the fateful decision to send an e-mail about a post she had just written to uber-blogger Guy Kawasaki. It was called "Open Letter to CXOs across the Corporate World," and it outlined all the glaring problems with corporations she had observed in a decade as a management consultant. Guy e-mailed her back right away and asked if she could expand on the post. So she stayed up until 1:30 a.m., finished it, and sent it back. The next morning, Guy blogged about it. "My stats went from 100 to 10,000 people a day. I had hundreds of e-mails and incoming links to my blog. As Malcolm Galdwell would say, it was my 'tipping point.'"

After that amazing exposure, Pam paid attention to key thinkers in her market. That included well-known bloggers as well as the average smart person with interesting things to say. She followed their blogs and commented frequently. It was a very organic process, based more on the pleasure of connecting with cool and interesting people rather than begging for links from "A-listers." The approach has resulted in wonderful and trusting relationships with some of the most influential people in her market, as well as personal connections with thousands of individuals interested in starting a business. "My blog has brought me all of my coaching and consulting clients, a five-figure book deal with a major publisher, and press coverage in the *New York Times, Wall Street Journal,* and *USA Today.*"

On average, Pam writes 3 to 4 posts a week and reads about 15 to 20 blogs a day. She tries to leave two to five comments a day, especially on the blogs of people who link to hers. "It's a sign of appreciation and respect, and I want them to know that I care about what they write and appreciate their support of my blog."

A Baker's Dozen of Content Sources and Ideas

The more variety of sources you use for your blog, the more you will look like an authority on your topic because readers will see your ability to take different materials and link them together under a common theme. Moreover, it shows that you're able to produce a lot of content, which tells the world that you have a lot to say on the topic, thereby adding to your expert status and increasing your networking gravity.

A great source of content is your own experience and observations of what's happening around you that relates to your topic. That's unique

content that no one else will have. In addition, here are 13 more ideas
and sources for blog content:

1. *Current headlines in newspapers or on news sites.* Comb through
   a newspaper or browse through a news Web site for a story you
   can spin to fit your topic. For example, when I travel overseas, I
   often read the *International Herald Tribune.* On one trip I came
   across a story about a scandal in South Korea where several
   notable public figures in government and academia were found
   to have lied about their credentials and were subsequently
   booted out of their jobs. They had gotten to the top of their
   professions claiming to have received degrees from prestigious
   universities and were now being exposed as liars. I immediately
   saw a connection to networking and how important it is to keep
   the trust of others, and I blogged about it.

   The news article can be about politics, entertainment,
   sports—it doesn't matter. Using stories from other fields can
   make your post more interesting. Write a couple of sentences on
   how this story is relevant to your blog topic, pick a quote or two
   to illustrate your point, and then link to the article online. Blogs
   love links. The more outbound links you have in your blog, the
   more of an authority you appear to be.

2. *Google Alerts.* Google Alerts is a monitoring service that will
   automatically e-mail you stories from the Web that contain
   keywords that you specify. Even if you don't blog, you'll want to
   set up a Google Alert with your name as the keyword so that
   you can be notified whenever it shows up in an article, press
   release, or blog post around the Internet.

   One of the great things about this service is the variety of
   source materials that Google uses both regionally and globally.
   In one alert, you might get links to articles in *CIO* magazine,
   TheStreet.com, and the *Daily Mail* in the United Kingdom, as
   well as a press release or two from PRWeb and a few blog
   entries from folks you've never heard of. The other great thing
   is that you can choose how often you receive alerts, whether
   daily, weekly, or whenever stories happen.

   I set up an e-mail folder for my alerts and will skim the
   headlines once a day or every other day. If something
   immediately catches my attention, I'll click on the link to read

the story and either take a few minutes to write a blog entry or keep the alert in the folder to write about later. If nothing looks interesting, I'll delete the alert.

3. *LinkedIn Answers.* We cover the business networking site LinkedIn in more detail in Chapter 12, but as a heads-up, the site has a feature called Answers where anyone in the community can ask a question and other members can answer. It's a fantastic place to get content ideas because you can see what questions people have about your topic. You can search by keyword or browse questions by category, by date posted, or by how many degrees away from you the questioner is in your network. You can get double the impact by answering the question on LinkedIn, and then posting the answer on your blog with a link to the original question. Repurposing content so that it's seen in as many places as possible is a very smart strategy.

4. *Other blogs.* Bookmark your favorite blogs and visit them regularly. When you're stuck for content, read the posts and comments to see if you can come up with an idea you can spin into an interesting entry for your blog, much like you would for a news article. Write a few sentences about why you chose the story, then create a link to it.

5. *Guest authors.* Invite other experts or people from your network to contribute a blog post, giving your blog readers another perspective on your topic. Guest posters in similar or related fields offer a great opportunity for others to get exposure to your audience and share their insights. If your guests also have blogs, you may be able to contribute a post yourself, and you may not even have to write it from scratch. You could take an existing post and add on a few sentences at the beginning or end to spin it slightly differently for that blog's audience.

6. *Interviews.* Interview authors and experts in your field, or talk to your own customers about their good experiences with your products or services. Write five to seven questions to ask, and share your interview in a simple question-and-answer format, which is easier to write than a narrative.

7. *Book reviews.* Read any good books lately? Readers visit your blog because they're interested in what you think. Telling them about a new book you've discovered or even sharing an opinion about one of the classics in your subject area is valuable. What

did you like about the book? How does it relate to your topic? What were the top three to five key takeaways?

8. *Survey results.* A poll gets readers to interact with your blog in an easy and anonymous way. It also gives you a sense of who your readers are and what they think. You can initiate a simple single-question poll where the answer choices are *yes*, *no*, and *not sure*. Then you can write a short blog entry to summarize the results. Another tactic is a more extensive multiple-question survey which could give you plenty of content ideas for many more blog entries.

9. *Lists.* Readers love lists because it gives them a finite number of things to read. Writers also like lists because it gives them a finite number of things to write. Start with a number, for example, 5, 7, or 10, then add a topic, like "secrets to better parenting" or "ways to build employee loyalty," depending on your expertise. Then start brainstorming the list. If you come up with more ideas, increase the number. If you run out of steam, decrease it.

10. *Questions to your blog readers.* You can initiate conversations directly and encourage readers to express what they think by writing a blog entry that asks an open-ended question. One question I once posed on my blog was, "What's the single biggest question you have about introducing yourself in networking situations?" Not only does this type of post encourage reader comments, but also the answers you receive are a wonderful source for future blog content. You can respond to one or more of the answers in future blog entries.

11. *Previous posts.* As you come across articles and stories that relate to a blog entry you've already written or if you'd just like to refocus your readers' attention on that area, you can revisit previous posts and update them with additional thoughts. Or, if you've learned new information that has changed your thinking on a topic you previously wrote about, write a new blog entry and link back to that original post.

12. *Reader comments.* Sometimes your readers will express a different viewpoint on your topic in the comments section of one of your posts. So if you're stuck for content, browse through the comments you've received to see if there might be a

slight twist on your topic that you can write about, or invite the person who posted the comment to be a guest blogger and submit a post to expand on his or her opinion.

13. *Videos and images.*   Guy Kawasaki, author of *The Art of the Start*, is great at this. His blog posts always have an interesting video, fun photos of the places he visited, a logo of the company he's writing about, or a cover graphic of the book he's reviewing. These add visual interest to your blog and make writing easier. All you have to do is comment on the video or the image, and you're done.

Walking the Fine Line between Personality and Getting Too Personal

As I've stressed in this chapter, it's important to be conversational in your blog and to show some personality. So it's fine to refer to things happening in your life if there are relevant lessons you can extract. I sometimes use a personal experience as a jumping-off point to talk about an interesting angle on networking. One Thanksgiving, I blogged about a debate I got into with my sister-in-law at the dinner table concerning whether women are better at networking than men.

Some people are more comfortable than others about sharing intimate details of their lives. And only you can decide what's appropriate based on your personality, your topic, and your audience. If you want to build credibility and authority, strive to present yourself in the best light possible, especially online where information not only spreads quickly but also lives on forever.

When you strike the right balance, blogs are a fantastic networking tool because on one side of the coin, they serve as an archive of the diverse thinking you've done and diverse sources you've collected on your topic. They allow you to share content and showcase your expertise to prospects, customers, associates, and the media. On the other side, they give the world a chance to see the different dimensions of your knowledge and personality, getting to know you, like you, and trust you without ever having to meet you. And in both instances, they enable an open dialogue that a static Web site just can't achieve.

CHAPTER 11

PUBLISH YOUR PERSPECTIVES

STAYING TOP OF MIND AND IN CIRCULATION WITH E-ZINES

> We do not write as we want but as we can.
>
> —*W. Somerset Maugham*

Keeping in touch with your network on a regular basis is an important part of networking effectively, because as much as we like to believe that people are thinking about us all the time, guess what? They're not. An opportunity might come across someone's desk that you would be perfect for, but if you're not top of mind at that moment, you won't hear about it.

When I started the networking group for independent consultants in 2001, I sent an e-mail to about 40 of my contacts letting them know about the group's first meeting, inviting them to attend, and asking them to forward the information to anyone who might be interested. I got this reply back from a former colleague:

RE: Free Agent Meeting 11/14

Hi Liz,

*How are you? I hope all is well. We might have a potential opportu-
nity for you. Please give me a call so we can discuss. I would love to
catch up too.*

Warm regards,
Elissa

When we spoke, she mentioned how funny it was to get my e-mail that
day because there was a project her company wanted to do but didn't have
the staff to do it, and I was exactly the right person to help. Though on a
completely unrelated topic, because my e-mail announcement landed in
her e-mail box that day, she immediately thought of me as a candidate.

That was the first time I realized the power of a well-timed e-mail
sent to a targeted group of people who knew me. How could I do this
more frequently, reach more people, and be in constant touch with my
network on a one-to-many basis? The answer? Launch an e-zine.

How E-zines Can Boost Your Networking

An e-zine pushes out information and keeps you in touch and on the
radar screens of hundreds, if not thousands, of customers, associates,
prospects, and colleagues on a regular basis. The word *e-zine* is short
for "electronic magazine" but is also known as an e-newsletter. It con-
tains short articles or tips in your area of expertise, is delivered by
e-mail to a list of subscribers, and is published at regular intervals, ideally no more than weekly and no less than monthly, experts say.

In the time it would take you to compose individual e-mails to a
handful of people, you can send one e-mail to your whole list, making
it an invaluable tool for smart networking.

E-zines Enable Passive Outreach

While that sounds like an oxymoron, passive outreach is important for
staying in touch with people without creating an obligation for them to
respond. While sending an individual e-mail is helpful when you are

requesting something specific from someone in your network, the purpose of an e-zine is to bring you top of mind on a regular basis without asking for anything in return. People can read your e-zine without feeling the obligation to respond the way a direct e-mail would.

E-zines Are a Platform to Share Your Expertise *Your* Way

Like your blog, your e-zine is an online communication tool to showcase your knowledge in a form that you're able to control. You're in charge of the look and feel of it, when you publish, and how often. When you write for other publications or when they write about you, you show up on their schedule, in their format, in their environment. While this coverage is helpful in reaching a wider audience, you still want to develop your own forum.

E-zines Give People an Easy Way to Connect with You

By hitting the "reply" button in your e-mail, your subscribers can send a message right back to you, without wasting time searching for your business card or wracking their brains to remember your Web site URL and then having to click around for your contact info. They can bring opportunities to you right when they think of them.

E-zines Provide Valuable Real Estate to Others

You can recommend the products and services of the people you know, like, and trust in your e-zine, giving them exposure to your audience and creating opportunities for connections within your network. In Bill Sobel's (Chapter 9) weekly e-zine for NY:MIEG he'll often give a plug for a colleague's upcoming event or congratulate a friend on an award, often prompting more registrations for the former, and forwarded e-mail kudos for the latter.

E-zines Get Your Content Out into the World

Publishing an e-zine forces you to create content on a regular basis, which will sharpen your thinking about your area of expertise. You may know your subject very well, but having to explain it in different ways to those who don't have the same knowledge base as you will make your ideas more relevant to more people. Plus, you'll develop a storehouse of content for speeches, articles, books, and other products. Last summer, I struck a deal with a Canadian government agency granting it permission to syndicate my e-zine articles for its internal career management Web site. The agency has made my articles available in English, and also translated them into French in accordance with Canada's Official Languages Act. Not only am I reaching a new audience of 40,000 people in a new country, but I'm also doing it in a whole new language! And now those French articles are available to me for resyndication to other French-speaking organizations.

E-zines Help Promote Your Business

While your e-zine shouldn't be completely promotional, people who are interested in your content will probably be interested in what you're doing. You can advertise new products and upcoming events and publicize your awards and accomplishments.

E-zines promote you and your business by promoting what you know rather than what you sell. They allow you to build a relationship with your audience over time with a strong, yet subtle, reminder of your expertise and value. The value that's added for your network is that you're continually relaying fresh insights about your area of expertise and how it might relate to the needs of others. It might inspire them to think differently about a problem, try out a new solution, or finally just take action and call you.

NETWORKING SUCCESS STORY 14
IGNITING ACTION WITH A STEADY STREAM OF REMINDERS
Patsi Krakoff, Psy.D., Cofounder
The Blog Squad
San Diego, California

Patsi Krakoff had been publishing newsletters since 1999. In 2002 she stopped publishing in print and now sends newsletters only by e-mail to her subscribers. As a psychologist working as a coach, she recognized the powerful marketing potential of newsletters, especially delivered electronically, as an adjunct to offline marketing.

Before she became half of The Blog Squad, she established Customized Newsletter Services, which she stills runs, to provide content and e-zines for executive coaches who didn't want to spend the time writing and publishing an e-zine. She uses her own monthly e-zine, *Newsletter Nuggets*, to connect with clients and let them know about new content for their publications. "It has been a major source of business for our e-zine and other consulting services. Frequent feedback from clients and subscribers indicates they are having great success with the e-zines we publish for them."

Mark Siegel, Bangkok, Thailand: "Since starting my e-zine 2 years ago I have signed up 40,000 subscribers all interested in knowing more about our golf in Thailand services. I religiously send out e-zines every 3 months and with each issue get around 10,000 US dollars in new orders. I post my old e-zines on my Web site in both html and PDF formats. The former is seen as new content by all the search engine spiders, thus helping our organic search rankings!"

Nancy Proffitt, West Palm Beach, Florida: "I have great results gaining new business today because people have been reading my e-zine as far back as three years ago. A longtime reader just referred me to Airbus North America after reading my February issue. Yes, I will be working with Airbus because of the indirect response to the e-zine. I love hearing from people who say, 'I know you, I love your e-zine. My boss or someone passed it on to me.'"

Dr. John N. Brennan: "My e-zine prompted an inactive account to become active. A publishing company bought my sales training, trained their salespeople, and were satisfied with the results. My attempts to win more business from them were not successful though my client remained on my mailing list. Two years later, an issue of my e-zine received a 'reply' e-mail from my client, asking me to call him. An article in the e-zine made him realize that his new sales strategy would require his reorganized sales organization to recommit itself to a consultative style of selling. Soon after I was back in the account. Had he not read my e-zine I doubt that he would have thought of the value of sales training and probably would not have contacted me."

All in all, Patsi believes that, "Publishing an e-zine is an important element for any professional's online marketing plan, but it's not the only tool. Smart professionals should also be using business blogs and other social networking tools to build their brand and reputation online. Each tool supports and extends the reach of the others. Each has a purpose and an audience."

Broadcasting at the Speed of E-mail:
How E-zines Differ from Blogs

There are some key differences between an e-zine and a blog that make having both desirable. In general, with an e-zine as with e-mail, content is distributed, pushing out information to your subscribers' in-boxes. With a blog as with a Web site, however, the content lives in one place on the Web. The blogging platform creates an automatic archive of your posts, making all your past entries easily accessible to visitors. While you could also create an archive of your e-zine articles, it's often a manual process and takes a few extra steps.

As we discussed in the previous chapter, you can mimic the push features of an e-zine with your blog by offering subscriptions to your e-mail feed so that each time you add a new post, an e-mail goes out to your blog subscribers. The downside of this is that if you post to your blog more often than weekly, your subscribers will hear from you too frequently. Your more sophisticated blog visitors can subscribe to your RSS feed instead so they'll be notified of new posts through an online feed reader, which is less intrusive than getting e-mail in their in-box.

Having both an e-zine and a blog allows you to show different facets of your business. The longer form of an e-zine article gives you more room for in-depth analysis on a topic, while the shorter form and linking nature of a blog post give you license to find an interesting online tidbit, comment quickly about it, and direct readers to the original source for more information.

Maintaining both an e-zine and a blog may take more time and work than you're prepared to put in, but you can easily save time and effort through cross-pollination and cross-promotion. Repackage content and post your e-zine articles to your blog to create an online archive, or add snippets of your recent blog posts to your latest e-zine to get your blog content more widely distributed to your whole e-mail list.

Blogs and e-zines serve different purposes, and having both will allow you to offer people more choices to get more of your content in the ways that they prefer, making opportunities flow more easily to you.

You Don't Need a Big List,
but You Do Need Permission

How do you communicate with people who visit your Web site, look around, and leave? Are you encouraging them to give you their e-mail address so you can build a relationship with them over time and keep in touch until they're ready to work with you?

Not doing this is like walking into a networking event, handing out your business card to everyone without saying a word, and leaving without getting any business cards in return. How are you supposed to follow up? Oh, you're going to wait for them to call you? Good luck with that. Let me know how that works out for you. Not everyone who visits your site or meets you in person will be a networking match for you ultimately, but you'll be better equipped to convert a greater percentage of them over time if you're able to open a channel of communication with them through e-mail.

The first step to making an e-zine work is to build your e-mail list. What's the best way to get someone onto your list? If you're interested in building a real relationship where they get to know, like, and trust you, you would ask their permission first. You wouldn't just show up in their in-boxes every week uninvited. Sending one e-mail to follow up after an event is fine and might include an invitation to join your list. But adding them automatically? Not cool. That could get you labeled a spammer and your e-mail address blacklisted across the Web.

Having access is not the same as having permission, says Seth Godin. In his bestselling book, *Permission Marketing*, he stresses that, "Frequency leads to awareness, awareness to familiarity, and familiarity to trust." But you first need permission to establish that process. Therefore, each person on your list should opt in explicitly to hear from you.

Building your list is the most important aspect of your e-zine. You can have the best e-zine in the world, but what is the value to you or anyone else if you have no one to send it to? How many subscribers you collect before you decide to launch your e-zine is up to you. I started with fewer than a hundred, which took me a long time to get to, but once I started publishing my e-zine, my list grew more quickly. My network started passing it along to other people they thought would also benefit from the information, and many subscribed to get their own copy directly.

The fastest way to grow your list is with a multipronged strategy:

- Put an opt-in form on your Web site and blog.
- Add an opt-in offer in your e-mail signature file.
- Whenever you speak, pass around a sign-up sheet to collect names and e-mail addresses, or at bigger events tell people to drop their business cards into a box if they'd like to get free tips by e-mail.
- Ask subscribers to forward your e-zine to their network.

You'll also want to offer potential subscribers an incentive, which Seth Godin says, gets them to pay attention and receive an explicit reward for the desired behavior of raising their hands to hear from you. Ideally, you want to give something that has value to them but is easy and cost effective for you to implement. This could be anything from a free article with your top 10 tips or an audio download of a recent presentation.

E-zine Basics

Once you've started to develop your opt-in e-mail list, you'll need to make some key decisions before launching your e-zine, although you can always adjust your approach later based on reader feedback.

How Often Should I Publish?

The right frequency depends on your audience, and you should determine this for yourself, but at least once a month is ideal for many people. Some companies publish weekly or twice a month, and you can always migrate there over time. For others, a quarterly schedule is a better fit for their business, although that means they're getting in front of their network only four times a year. If one of your e-mails gets caught in a spam filter or happens to land in people's e-mail boxes when they're on vacation, then they won't hear from you for at least six months.

How Long Should My E-zine Be?

It's best to start out simply with perhaps one feature article and a short blurb about your company. If you include too many sections and have too much to write for each issue, you'll get overwhelmed and may have a hard time getting your e-zine out consistently. Some marketers say that a shorter e-zine published more frequently is better than a longer e-zine published less frequently, but again, that depends on your topic and your audience.

Text, HTML, or PDF Format?

Each has its pluses and minuses. HTML e-mails are more eye-catching than text because you can include graphics, colors, and different fonts, but text e-mails tend to have higher deliverability because they don't get trapped in spam filters as often. PDF newsletters look better when printed out than HTML ones, but the downside is that you need to send them as an attachment to an e-mail, and anyone concerned about viruses probably won't open it. Whichever format you decide on, be sure to make a copy available online through your Web site or blog so your content can live and be found on the Web.

How Do I Manage My List?

Don't try to send out your e-zine through your regular e-mail program like Outlook. To manage spam, some ISPs have a limit to the number of people you can e-mail to at one time. Plus, as your list grows, it becomes harder to manually add new subscribers and remove those who want to unsubscribe. The best way to manage your e-mail list is to sign up with a list management service like Constant Contact or AWeber to handle the process from start to finish, including confirming opt-ins, managing subscribes and unsubscribes, publishing in HTML and text formats, and distributing your e-zine to your list. You still have to write the content, but they take care of the logistics.

Can E-Zines Work for Company Employees?

E-zines can be great tools for salespeople to provide value-added content to their clients and prospects and stay in touch with them on a regular basis. Other types of employees, however, might get bigger impact for their efforts from other networking tools such as industry groups or even some social networking sites.

Ideas for Generating Content

The same ideas and sources that inspire your blog content (Chapter 10) can also be applied to your e-zine, such as current events, interviews with industry experts and clients, and reader questions. Here are some additional ones:

- *Answer subscriber mail.* When your e-zine subscribers e-mail you with questions, save those questions in a folder and browse through them when you are looking for content ideas. You can write an article inspired by a question, but I often find it easier to include the actual question in the story, which I may edit for style or grammar. Then I type my answer below it. If I have permission, I'll include the person's name or initials, or change the name if the questioner wishes to remain anonymous.
- *Swap articles with other e-zine publishers.* Find other experts who also publish e-zines and ask if they would be willing to exchange articles. You can publish one of theirs, and they can publish one of yours. By doing this, you're essentially cross-promoting each other to your respective audiences.
- *Expand a blog entry.* I like to keep my blog entries to fewer than 300 words, but for my e-zine I may go as high as 900 words. So, if I have more to say on a topic I started to write about on my blog, I might write a short summary for my blog and expand it into a longer article for my e-zine.
- *Reprint articles from article directories.* On sites like EzineArticles. com, experts from across the Web can submit articles that anyone can republish for free. The catch is that you cannot alter the article in any way, including title, text, or author information, and you must attribute the article properly to the author, meaning you can't put your byline on it. Though several of my own articles have been picked up by others, personally, I would tend to choose this option for my own e-zine only in a pinch. I'd prefer to use that real estate to invite contributions from my network instead.

- *Outsource it completely.* You can hire companies like Patsi Krakoff's Customized Newsletter Services, mentioned in this chapter's Networking Success Story 14, to create an e-zine for you, including articles and graphics, and send it out to your list on a monthly basis. It's a great solution if you don't have the time or the infrastructure to commit to this level of communication on a regular basis.

Easy E-zine Alternatives:
Other Ways to Keep in Touch with E-mail

If you have time for only a blog or an e-zine but not both, I would recommend investing your time in the blog since that networking tool is truly available 24/7 from anywhere in the world. Even if you don't publish a regular e-zine, it's still worthwhile to build an opt-in e-mail list using the strategies we covered earlier so that you have some type of broadcasting tool to connect with your network on a mass level through e-mail.

Once you have the list, an alternative to a regular e-zine is to send e-mails on an ad hoc basis to forward articles you've written for other publications, for example, or to announce new products, awards, or company changes. Another option is to send holiday wishes by e-mail for whatever holidays you choose. However, there should be no promotion whatsoever. Keep your holiday greetings pure. Your e-mail message will still be an effective reminder of who you are, but it will be more welcome without the overt marketing.

NETWORKING SUCCESS STORY 15
SENDING APPROPRIATELY TARGETED ONE-OFF E-MAILS
Ramon Gil, Creative Director
Fresh Concentrate
New York, New York

Whenever Ramon Gil gets a truly amusing chain e-mail or has some tidbit that he thinks people would get a kick out of, he goes through his address book to see who would really relate to it or enjoy it. "I especially include people I haven't been in touch with in a while, even taking the time to go through the stacks of business cards on my desk. It's a great excuse to get back in touch with people who may be potential business leads for you."

During the holidays, Ramon wrote a poem called "'Twas the Night before Christmas, 2007" about the endless presidential debates that were going on, and he sent it out to over 600 people on his Constant Contact mailing list. Shortly after that e-mail, he got five new projects: (1) a company that accepted his offer to advise them on finding a Web developer decided it was better off with him; (2) a consultant whom he had worked with years earlier and was happy to get back in touch immediately gave him a publication to design; (3) a previous client who decided to let his company do all the brochures for its health network; (4) the husband of a friend whose medical practice needed a Web site; and (5) the ex-husband of a friend who needed a whole branding and marketing package for his contracting company.

"Your network only works if you stay in touch. And appropriately targeted mass e-mails are a great way to do it."

CHAPTER 12

LEVERAGE ONLINE COMMUNITIES
EXTENDING YOUR REACH WITH SOCIAL NETWORKING

> Seek those who find your road agreeable, your personality and mind stimulating, your philosophy acceptable, and your experiences helpful. Let those who do not, seek their own kind.
>
> —*Jean-Henri Fabre*

Social networking sites are online communities in which users can find and interact with other users who share common interests. The beauty of social networking is that it extends the boundaries of time and geography in your networking, so you have more freedom about when, where, and how you network. Rather than getting dressed up to be at a certain place at a certain time, you can network with people all over the world whenever you want.

The ease with which social networks allow us to connect with others and stay connected without leaving our homes and offices makes them a vital tool for smart networking. But keep in mind that online networks *enable* relationships, not take the place of them. There's still a person behind that online profile, and all the rules of effective face-to-face networking still apply. In other words, lead with value, help when you can, don't promote yourself overtly, and choose carefully whom, what, and how you ask for something. All the skills we covered in Part II will definitely come in handy.

The social networking landscape is constantly changing, and by the time you read this, there will be new sites and tools on the scene. The goal of this chapter is to outline how best to incorporate online networking to enhance your overall networking results, rather than focus on the sites themselves and describe all of their features. Once you understand how to approach online networking in general, you can pick and choose the right tools to integrate into your repertoire.

However, there are a number of sites that have critical mass right now and should be part of your overall networking plan. For the busy business professional or entrepreneur, using a *professional* networking site and a *personal* networking site in combination, like LinkedIn and Facebook, can be very powerful and will be our primary focus here. One other site we'll touch on briefly because of its increasing importance to those marketing their business or building their personal brand is Twitter.

Why LinkedIn + Facebook?

If you're a professional, you want to be on LinkedIn. With over 25 million registered users from around the world, as of August 2008, presenting their work experience and educational information in an online résumé format, the tone on the site is all business. You won't find photos of anyone in face paint at a football game or lots of the bells and whistles you'll see on other sites. What you will find are professionals who want to connect with other professionals in a number of ways. First, by sending invitations to be part of each other's networks; second, by asking and answering business-related questions from other members of the community; and third, by contacting each other directly for job and business opportunities.

While LinkedIn shows the world who you are as a professional, Facebook lets you show more of who you are as a person and engage with other members in less serious ways. You can list favorite quotes, books, and songs, upload videos and photos from events, and challenge your friends to quizzes. On my own Facebook page I've posted a TripAdvisor map with all the places I've traveled to highlight what a travel bug I am, as well as the results of the movie quizzes I've taken (a perfect score for "Celebs with No Makeup"!) to show my interest in film and entertainment.

This extra information is important in networking because it adds another layer of understanding of who you are as a person and what you're interested in. It's easier to spark a connection with someone when we share something in common, because immediately, we have a topic to converse around. But don't think of Facebook as just for your fun side. More and more people are figuring out how to leverage it for professional uses too, like announcing a new product, marketing a seminar, or building their e-mail lists.

As a personal choice, I do prefer Facebook over its larger rival MySpace. With more than 90 million active users as of August 2008, and more than half of them outside of college, Facebook is a big enough venue for the kind of networking that most of us want to do. Bebo, which is popular outside the United States, is another option. Certainly, if you have the time and the interest, explore these as well as smaller niche sites in your industry. E.Factor, a social network that also offers in-person networking options, is one of the most interesting examples. Ask your friends and colleagues which sites they use. Remember though, whether online or in person, it's not important how many communities you join, but how active you are in them, so choose your mix of sites wisely.

Think of your LinkedIn page as your professional persona. How you present yourself to the world during work hours. Your Facebook page is your social persona—how you present yourself to the world after work and on weekends—so you can be much more playful and creative there. You still want to appear balanced and stable, of course. Keep in mind that the information you post on these sites can be seen by other members, and some details may be open to the Web public at large. Don't post anything you wouldn't want your boss or your mother to see, or the *New York Times* to write about.

So, let's discuss the business benefits of these social networking sites both for active networking and for passive networking.

Benefits for Active Networking

Social networking sites can facilitate many of the outreach functions you would perform in offline networking.

Prospecting

You can search by keyword for users on the site with specific backgrounds or interests that appeal to you. That means if you're looking for a potential business partner or job candidate with certain qualifications to fill a need in your company, chances are you'll be able to find that person somewhere on the site. And you're not limited by geography as you would be with in-person networking. The whole world is open to you.

Communication

Social networking sites open up lines of communication that would be harder to do in person. If you're hesitant to approach strangers at networking events, especially if they're well-known, you'll have a much easier time starting a dialogue with them online. I've found that people in these communities tend to be very friendly and open. Part of the reason may be that they can click over to your profile and see who you are. You're not anonymous to them as you would be in an e-mail because they can see the person behind the message, making the whole networking process more transparent.

Research

Social networking can warm people up to each other, taking some of the edge off and making meeting in person a lot more comfortable when and if it happens. Before I meet with someone for the first time, I might look them up on LinkedIn or Facebook and see what we have in common. Perhaps we know the same people or have similar hobbies. Being able to find common links helps you form a bond with someone more quickly. You could try to accomplish this research on Google, but often the search results can surface a lot of extraneous material, so it's much easier to go straight to a social networking site to get this information.

Thought Leadership

Online networking sites also allow you to showcase your expertise. LinkedIn has a section called Answers where members post questions on business topics and other members provide answers. Both sides win in this case because the person asking the question gets a diverse range of insight from the community, while the members who post answers have a forum to show what they know about the topic. On Facebook, you can also share content by feeding your blog posts into your profile page through RSS feeds and posting videos and photos related to your business. The good news is that all your information, including your profiles, questions, answers, comments, recommendations, and so on, is always available 24/7 to those in the community.

Benefits for Passive Networking

While online networking can make parts of your active networking easier and more expansive, what I find even more powerful is how it enables passive networking, being in the game for people to reach out to you.

Discoverability

Your profile can be viewed by other members of the community from anywhere in the world 24/7, and, depending on how much information you make available for casual browsing, they can get to know you on their own without any time required on your part. Your online profile and Web site should work together so those searching for you in the community can click over to your Web site for more detailed information about your business, while those browsing your Web site can jump to your online profile for more detailed information about you as a person. Your profiles can be effective marketing tools to attract potential business opportunities automatically.

Availability

Online networking enables the long tail. You don't know where the demand to network with you is going to come from, but you're always "in stock" when the demand arrives. You don't have to show up at a specific place at a specific time and be limited to interacting only with those in the room. Online, anyone can get to know you anytime, and there's unlimited inventory of you to go around. You can even multiply the distribution of your profile through friends and connections. Your public profile is accessible through the profiles of those you are linked to, provided your friends enable their connections to be viewed. Again, the more places you can be found, the more people can network with you.

Passive Job Search

Passive networking is perfect for those who have jobs but are open to moving around for the right opportunity. Increasingly, recruiters prefer to use LinkedIn to find passive job candidates over traditional job search sites that tend to attract more active job seekers. If you're interested in career advancement, you want to be sure you can be found when the right opportunity comes along. You also want to be sure to start building both your online and offline networks to give you more options once you're ready to make a change on your own.

Lasting Connections

Passive networking also includes staying connected to your contacts even when they move around. That means you never have to lose track of former classmates and colleagues because their work e-mail address or phone number is no longer valid. As long as they are an active member of one of the communities you belong to, you'll always be able to keep in touch. Start connecting with your colleagues online right now so that you can always stay connected. You never know when you'll need their help or vice versa.

NETWORKING SUCCESS STORY 16
WINNING OFFICE WITH A WINNING ONLINE STRATEGY
Mike Germano, President and Creative Director
Carrot Creative
New York, New York

Mike Germano embarked on his political career at the age of 23, two months after graduating from college. As a graduate of the class of 2005 and one of the first groups of students able to utilize Facebook and MySpace, he was well-versed in the power of social platforms and decided to leverage this knowledge to win a seat on Hamden, Connecticut's town council.

"For my campaign, I maximized efforts toward my district's student constituency through Facebook by utilizing search tools to find politically like-minded students in my networks; locating students in my voting district through searchable housing information; and creating support groups and fund-raising events that allowed for mass messaging."

At that time, Facebook was regulated to only school networks, so Mike utilized MySpace to reach the rest of his net-savvy constituents by enlisting the assistance and support of any users/groups located within his town and personally connecting with these users through constant messaging.

By utilizing both Facebook and MySpace, Mike was able to run a standard grassroots campaign and a "virtual door-to-door" campaign simultaneously, thus capturing a majority of the district's support yet maintaining efficient allocation of resources. Mike won his election by a landslide, making him one of the youngest politicians in Connecticut history.

His commitment to social media efforts continued through his term as he engaged all his affiliated Facebook/MySpace groups, maintained constant correspondence on local blogs, and pursued town policies that created more government transparency through social media engagement.

"My term as a town councilman ended in 2007, and I'm now head of a social media marketing/design firm."

Getting Started Isn't Hard

The best way to get started with online networking is to follow the same three-step process for successful networking offline: prepare, connect, and strengthen.

1. Prepare

Because users search a community based on profile information, the first thing you want to do is fill out your profile as completely as possible from a professional standpoint. Put in a description of your current position or business, past employment information, and your school affiliations. Use keywords in your profile related to your function (e.g., copywriting, marketing communications) and industry (e.g., financial services, private wealth management, etc.) so that you'll appear in the appropriate search results. Upload a photo if possible so people can tell you apart from the other members in the community with the same name and you become a real person to those considering connecting with you. Also, an interesting picture can draw people to you as they're browsing profiles. Once your profile is up, you're ready to connect.

On Facebook, there is a lot of room to share personal interests like hobbies and favorite musical groups. It's important to fill out some of this information so people can learn a bit of who you are as a person, but don't get bogged down here. You can always add more to your profile later.

2. Connect

Don't be surprised if you start getting invitations to connect right away as some of your contacts already on the site have preloaded their address books and been alerted that you're now a member. Accept those invitations and then look around on their list of contacts and friends, and invite those you know and those who look interesting to connect with you directly.

Search for people in the network you already know. You can search for individuals by their first and last name, but sometimes that can produce a very long list of people with the same name that you then have to cull. Sometimes it's easier to search organizations instead, like former employers and universities, for people you know, as well as browsing the friends of friends you're already connected to.

Both LinkedIn and Facebook allow you to craft a personal message to go out with your invitation to connect which I will often do, especially if I'm introducing myself to someone who doesn't know me. You wouldn't just give your card out to people without introducing yourself and then expect them to figure out why they should talk to you. I always appreciate when someone takes the time to personalize a message. Here's a recent one I got: *"Hi Liz, my name is Travis Greenlee, we are mutual friends of Stu M. Looks like you are up to some BIG things, me too! Let's be Facebook friends and get to know each other."* That's all it takes.

You might also consider joining a few networks. On Facebook, these have been set up by region, company, and school. To join a company or school network, you'll need a valid e-mail address from that institution. So if your current employer has a company network, join it now because if or when you leave, you'll be shut out.

You can also find groups to join based on your interests. Search by keyword or group name, although because there are so many of them, it can be difficult and time consuming to wade through the search results. I like to take shortcuts by looking through my friends' profiles to see which groups they belong to. What are friends for if they can't help you sift through information?

3. Strengthen

Setting up your profile and linking up with a few friends and groups is the minimum you should do to get started. Your ongoing participation is what will help strengthen your presence on the site and give you more results. Set aside a few minutes each week to extend and accept invitations, and on Facebook, update your status to give all your friends a brief glimpse into what you're doing.

Just about any activity you do on LinkedIn or Facebook will generate a headline in your friends' news feeds on their personal home pages on these social networking sites. Every time you update your status, change your profile picture, or add a new connection, you're popping up on their radar screens. In addition, there are a number of high-impact activities you should find time to fit into your schedule:

Show Your Thought Leadership

On LinkedIn, devote some time to answering questions in your area of expertise to become known as a thought leader. When I interviewed Jason Alba, author of *I'm on LinkedIn, Now What???*, he recommended that even corporate types use these sites to start branding themselves as subject matter experts. You can browse the list of open questions posed by your extended network, drill down into a specific category, or search by keyword. Be sure to answer the questions thoughtfully and add to the conversation. Be careful about promoting yourself in your answer, keeping in mind that you'll usually sell yourself more effectively with content than with advertising. In answering a question about finding a Web developer, for example, writing something like, "Here's a link to an article I wrote that highlights the five things to watch out for when hiring a Web developer," is better than, "I have the best Web development team in the Northeast, here's a link to our Web site."

Leverage the LinkedIn community as well for questions you have, anything ranging from recommendations for a vendor to thoughts on tackling a particular business challenge in management, sales, or operations. But be sure to keep it general. You don't want to reveal any insider information or specific names. Members answer questions because they like to help and get a chance to show what they know, and you can begin to develop relationships with those who seem particularly helpful and knowledgeable.

Beef Up Your Profile

It's generally better to have more information available about you in your profile than less. This provides multiple hooks that people can grasp onto. If you have a blog, syndicate it to your profile page. That way, every time you write a new entry, the headline will appear on your page and on your friends' news feeds automatically. If you have a product demo or a clip of a speech you gave, that could help people learn more about you and your business. If you're not tech savvy, get a friend or your Webmaster to help you.

Make sure you're cross-promoting everything you're doing online across each of your online platforms so that you can leverage your efforts as much as possible. For example, you should add links to your blog, Web site, and e-zine subscription form from your profile so people can easily access other information about you. The information is already out there; you spent time creating it; you might as well use it everywhere you can.

Extend Your Offline Relationships

After meeting in person, invite people to connect with you on Facebook or LinkedIn so you can keep in touch and continue to get to know each other over time in an unobtrusive way. Keep in mind that everyone will have a different policy about whose invitations they will accept on different social networking sites. Some folks want to preserve Facebook as a place to connect with their long-term friends. Others might be more open with Facebook but limit LinkedIn contacts to people they've actually worked with. Respect whatever policy they have and don't take it personally if your invitation isn't accepted.

Keep in Touch with Contacts

See who's having a birthday or who's announced a job change or a life change. This is a great excuse to send your congratulations, and it's something you would probably do in the offline world anyway if the information were at your fingertips. Social networking sites give you easy access to that information, so use the tools to your advantage.

Okay, So What about Twitter?

To help increase awareness about your business and attract people into your network who are interested in what you do, Twitter can be an excellent addition to your social networking toolkit. In posts of 140 characters or less that are broadcast to the Twitter pages of the folks who've chosen to follow you, you can offer advice, share a resource, broadcast a success, or ask for help. By initiating and contributing to conversations, you can rapidly build relationships with people all over the world who can help spread your message.

So what's the catch? Unlike LinkedIn and Facebook where the information on your profile page is all about you, your accomplishments, and interests, and that's okay, the primary information on your Twitter page is your last 20 posts. The primary way then for people to judge you as a potential networking partner and choose whether or not to follow you is not by your background but by how you're engaging with the community based on what you've posted. Are you constantly promoting your own Web site and blog or are you linking to other helpful resources too? Are you talking about yourself predominantly or are you helping and supporting others? When you are talking about yourself, are you saying interesting things?

Networking successfully on Twitter requires balancing diverse objectives of promoting your business, sharing personal insights, and listening and responding to conversations going on in the community. It may not be right for everybody, but if you do join, plan on posting multiple times a day to stay visible and make sure you're covering all of these bases. It takes time and thought, but if you're willing to make the investment, you'll expand your universe of contacts, build deeper relationships, and gain more support for your endeavors.

NETWORKING SUCCESS STORY 17
TWITTERING ON SUCCESS
Laura "@Pistachio" Fitton, Principal
Pistachio Consulting Inc.
Boston, Massachusetts

Laura Fitton is lucky to have a rapidly expanding network of 5,000-plus (August 2008) "loose ties" with brilliant, engaged, interesting people from all over the world. It took her less than 18 months to build it.

Laura's job is to make presentations "rock more." In March 2007, after more than two years of time off for maternity, she relaunched her business in Boston. "I was all but homebound with two kids under two and no childcare. I dove into blogging and social networking, and pretty soon I started hearing about something called Twitter."

Twitter is a deceptively simple social networking, publishing, and community Web application. You post short notes of 140 characters or less for your "followers" to read, and you read the "Tweets" of people you've elected to follow. "It sure looked pointless to me. Over time and with a lot of guidance from people like Chris Brogan (@ChrisBrogan on Twitter), however, it's become the single most important force in my life and business success."

Laura stumbled into close personal friendships with incredibly accomplished people. Through Twitter, people get a direct sense of how Laura's mind works by reading the media, ideas, and resources she publishes. Collaboration, connection, mentoring, inspiration, and untold opportunity result from this "tapping into others' brains" to share ideas, spirit, and enthusiasm. Effortlessly. With thousands.

"Now I'm in a surreal position where people I consider my heroes are interviewing me to analyze why this has worked so well and what lessons to draw from it. I sat on a panel for Guy Kawasaki and have speaking invitations for Switzerland, Germany, and California. My last half dozen new business inquiries are directly attributable to my Twitter community. It's silly, but the other day the executive producer of Curb Your Enthusiasm, Tim Gibbons, helped me with my BlackBerry."

Laura shares her ideas by posting text, video, audio, photos, and links, using an array of applications like Seesmic, Qik, and Utterz. Whenever she needs help, advice, ideas, feedback, or just someone to chat with, she posts to Twitter. In a very real sense, she is never alone.

The Challenges of What Comes After

Of course, there is no such thing as a free lunch. While online networking allows you to connect with people all over the world with similar interests, simply having a profile on a site won't automatically translate into new business any more than simply showing up at a networking event or paying your membership dues to a networking group will. It may happen, but you'll have to be proactive and know the process to follow to reach your objectives. Be prepared to deal with some of the challenges.

The Learning Curve

As with any new technology, there's a learning curve to get set up and then figure out where to focus your time. You also have to deal with the learning curves of others in the community. Many people on these sites don't really know how to use them effectively for business networking. Because traditional in-person networking has been around a long time, when people attend events, they have some idea of what to do, even if they may not feel comfortable doing it. They know they're supposed to circulate, initiate conversations with others, learn about what they do, exchange business cards, and determine what follow-up is appropriate. The process isn't as defined with online networking. It's more self-directed and new to many people, so many stumble around trying to figure it all out. Whom should I network with? How do I start an online conversation? What applications should I be using?

The silver lining to having to learn something new is that there are people in the community willing to help. When I lamented on my blog last year that I had joined Facebook but couldn't figure out what to do next, social media superhero and cofounder of PodCamp Chris Brogan came to my rescue. Since then, a steady stream of books and resources has rushed in to demystify the different alternatives and help guide the way for new users. Because new information is being developed all the time, visit www.smartnetworking.com for the latest recommendations.

The Time Trade-Off

While online networking does save you time from traveling to events and enduring another rubber chicken lunch, you still need to be active within the community to have a meaningful experience. If you let your profile languish or don't do any outreach, you'll become more invisible as more people join the site. So don't be fooled. It can take just as much work, sometimes more, to cultivate your online network as it does your offline network, especially in the beginning.

Offline you can get people's attention by standing in front of them. When you meet someone at a networking event, you've both devoted that time on your calendars to be there. And within a five-minute conversation, you can gauge the potential to build a mutually beneficial relationship. A lot of it comes down to chemistry, which you can more easily assess face-to-face than virtually.

Extending invitations, accepting invitations, responding to messages, and updating your status all take time. And it's just as easy to spend two hours posting and answering questions on LinkedIn or reading and responding to Tweets on Twitter as it is to spend two hours at a networking event. Just as you would set aside time to attend a weekly breakfast or monthly event in your offline networking, you should set aside time—and set time limits—for online networking too.

One way to save a lot of time on Facebook is to ignore the vast majority of applications on the site, which can clutter your page and make it hard for people to pick out the really important information about you. In other words, don't bother sending vampire bites or accepting invitations to get hugged—unless you really want to.

The Dizzying Array of Places to Belong

The biggest advantage I've seen to being an early adopter on a social networking site is to grab the ideal user name. Other than that, I doubt you'll miss much if you show up a little later. It's not like arriving early at a live event when the room is quieter and you don't have to struggle above the din to have a productive conversation. With online networking, you can come into the conversation anytime. In fact, from a time-saving standpoint, it's clearly to your advantage to wait until there is a critical mass of your peers, potential customers, and experts who've already mapped out the territory. In other words, it doesn't pay to be Lewis and Clark; you've got plenty of other things to do.

On the flip side, though, don't expect to join a community and begin asking for things immediately. That works even less well in online networking than it does for in-person networking. Plan to spend time familiarizing yourself with the site and building visibility in the right way by following the guidelines we've already talked about.

Because the social networking space continues to evolve, it's worth keeping one ear open for new sites that people in your network are using. If you find that a significant number of colleagues are gravitating toward a particular site, ask them these questions to see if it's worthwhile to join:

1. *What's the focus of the site?*   Participating on another general networking site may not necessarily give you anything new. However, if a site is specific to your industry and is an active, vibrant community where members are regularly congregating to share ideas and generate opportunities for one another in your profession, it may be worth investigating.
2. *Who's on the site?*   What kinds of people and how many? As I said, there's usually no advantage to being an early adopter. As long as you can become involved quickly once you determine whether the site is right for you, you really don't need to start early.
3. *What can I do on the site?*   How might a new site help you network differently from the other sites you're already on? If the site allows for more multimedia content, for example, that might be valuable real estate to leverage to host other types of information that allow you to showcase your expertise such as videos, podcasts, chats, slideshows, and the like.

While I put the LinkedIn + Facebook combination with an option for Twitter as a stake in the ground, you may find that a different blend of tools works better for you. For instance, blogger and social media entrepreneur Jeff Pulver wrote in *BusinessWeek* last year that since he was relying more and more on Facebook for his business networking, he didn't see the need to stay in LinkedIn at all. And now, he's created unique live Facebook events all over the world, bringing people together for "real-time social networking."

You may want to devote some time each month to explore new social networking tools, regardless of whether you decide to eventually use them or not. Smart networking is also about continuous improvement and always trying to find ways to increase results without increasing effort. And who knows? Maybe you'll find something that works perfectly for your profession and personality.

Online Networking Is *Not* a Magic Bullet

Just as with in-person networking, you can't expect results overnight. It takes just as much time and care to develop relationships online as it does in person. In fact, some people make the mistake of believing they can be more informal, blasé, and take shortcuts when they're connecting with others online.

Whether online or in person, you still need to make a positive first impression and be able to communicate effectively. And sometimes the written word can be more challenging than the spoken one. For example, a comment you meant to be tongue-in-cheek might come across as obnoxious if people can't hear the tone of your voice. Because your full personality won't come through in the words in your profile or your online communications, meaning that no one can see your body language or hear the sincerity in your voice, you have to be more careful about what you say and make sure it can't be misconstrued.

If you have trouble networking in person, social networking won't solve all your problems. While there are certainly many benefits to networking online in terms of expanding your contacts across geographies, starting conversations, and staying in touch more easily, you still have to be able to relate to people on a personal level. Showing that you're interested in *them*, not just in what they can do for *you* is just as important in this medium as it is in any other.

PART IV

CONNECTING ONE, TWO, THREE

TAKING ACTION WITH YOUR OWN SMART NETWORKING PLAN

CHAPTER 13

READY, SET, ACTION

A ONE-PAGE PLAN
THAT WORKS FOR YOU

> Start by doing what's necessary, then what's possible,
> and suddenly you are doing the impossible.
>
> —*St. Francis of Assisi*

The two groups of people I had in my mind while writing this book represent the person I was—the reluctant networker unsure of how to get started and with more than a few fears to overcome—and the person I am today—the busy entrepreneur always looking for a productivity edge to get more done in less time. If you've ever been averse to networking, I hope the strategies and success stories you've read so far have inspired you. If multitasking is more the rule rather than the exception for you, I hope you've discovered some ways to maximize the impact of your networking efforts so you can get in and get out.

Whichever group you fall into, or if you're somewhere else on the spectrum, you don't need to, and really shouldn't, attempt all the connection strategies in this book all at once. There just wouldn't be enough hours in the day to fit in all of these networking activities *and* do your job *and* have a life. I don't expect that of myself, and I don't expect it from you either. But you do have to invest something. You'll have to do some things differently and perhaps push beyond your comfort zone. And most important, you'll have to take action. As a reward for getting all the way to this chapter, I want to show you the best way to apply what you've learned so that you can take effective action immediately.

While you're welcome to jump in anywhere and start in on any of the strategies I covered in Part II or III that resonate with you most, I propose a more goal-oriented approach. I'm a pragmatist. Hearing the advice "Just get out there and start networking" is like hearing air-traffic control say, "Just get up there and start flying." That's all well and good until you run out of fuel somewhere short of where you want to be. Smart networking isn't about logging in hours in the cockpit; it's about doing the things that help you reach your goal in the most effective and efficient way possible. It all starts with a coherent plan.

Get with the Program

A plan is a specific program for getting from point A to point B. One of my biggest strengths is helping people and companies put together simple, strategic game plans for their businesses that bring an overall goal to reality through clear and specific actions. By bringing that skill to networking, I've been able to help many professionals save time, save money, and connect with confidence.

The most important part of a plan is knowing where you want to end up. Then you can take stock of where you are and determine the best way to proceed. I know that planning scares people who prefer to live more spontaneously. If you have time to network more serendipitously, then stop reading here. But if you're a busy professional who wants to use your time wisely, then keep going.

A plan forces you to do some thinking in advance to determine what's important and why you're doing it. It's like logging in your flight plan with the control tower. Once you're clear in your mind where you want to go, you'll be more effective at relaying that message to others and securing their cooperation to help you get there. You'll be proactive instead of reactive.

Don't worry that you'll have to stick rigidly to your plan. It's important to be able to read the weather patterns ahead and make adjustments as necessary, but you're always aware of your ultimate destination.

I believe that planning shouldn't be complicated and that it shouldn't take a long time. I also believe in putting a plan in writing. It makes your plan concrete, and everything you need is in one place for easy reference.

Developing Your Plan: Some Key Considerations before You Start

Smart networking starts by identifying what works for you, based on your goals, your timeline, and your strengths. You can continue to do the things you enjoy, but you may have to add on other things if doing so will help you reach your goal more quickly.

Your Purpose Drives Your Plan

The foundation of a smart networking plan starts with your purpose, the current objective you wish to achieve in your business or career. There are a vast number of networking activities you can participate in and people you can meet, but without defining your purpose first, how will you know where to start? How will you know what will be most effective? How do you keep from spinning your wheels? Without that clarity, you'll waste time doing the wrong things and not spend enough time on the right things.

Where people go wrong is when they start immediately on the actions—showing up at events, opening a LinkedIn account—without thinking of the bigger picture and with goals that are vague at best. Their efforts are diffused across so many different areas that nothing seems to click. Not only that, but because the activities they choose will determine the people they will meet, if they choose the wrong activities, they'll meet the wrong people and networking will be a struggle all around. So you can do this the hard way and end up lost, or you can make networking more effortless and effective by starting off in the right place: with your purpose.

Timeline Matters

Think in advance about a time frame for your plan. If you have a short deadline because you need to find a job in three weeks or you'll miss a mortgage payment, then that will change the whole landscape of your plan. You'll have to be more proactive with outreach and direct contact. Hopefully, you won't find yourself in such a desperate situation because it will be more difficult to have productive, low-key conversations when the clock is ticking. And while your contacts will sense your anxiety, there may not be much they can do to help, and that will put you both on edge.

That's why, ideally, you should start building and strengthening relationships as early as you can, long before you need to, to develop your skills and expand your contact base. The less urgent a deadline you have, the more activities you can put on autopilot. You'll have time to attract better opportunities and not have to take the first job or project that comes along. With a longer time frame, perhaps you'd join a committee of your industry trade association to start augmenting your network outside your current sphere of contacts and increasing the number of sources for potential opportunities.

Your Preferences Matter Too

Do you love to write? Do you like meeting one-on-one? Does the thought of leading a volunteer organization really appeal to you? Your preferences will play a key role in determining your best actions for your one-page plan. If you include activities in your plan that you like to do, you'll be more likely to do them.

But don't be afraid to experiment either. By testing out some strategies you've never tried before, you may discover some that work even better for you. At times you may also need to venture beyond your preference zone in order to build relationships with certain people or reach more people more quickly. While you may not like to go to conferences, for example, that may be the best place to connect with an industry superstar or a big population of your target prospects.

Remember too that one person's joy is another person's chore. Just before I finished writing this book, I had lunch with a friend who asked for a sneak preview of the networking techniques I was recommending. I told him, "One thing that's really worked for me is writing a blog." He rolled his eyes and said, "Ugh, that sounds like too much work." I smiled because here he was doing all his networking one-on-one and face-to-face. To me, *that* seemed like too much work.

Creating Your Customized One-Page Plan

Here are the steps for crafting your own smart networking one-page plan that is simple enough to put together in under 30 minutes, yet powerful enough to keep you moving forward consistently on your most important goal. Why one page? Two reasons: I want to force you to prioritize, and I want to keep you focused at the same time. By limiting the space for the number of connections and activities, you have to think in advance which ones to work on first. Plus the fewer pages you need to fill out, the less time you'll need, and the easier it will be to refer to your plan regularly.

1. Purpose

It's very easy to avoid networking if you don't feel you have a reason to do it. But if you know you need to, having a specific answer to the question of "Why do I want to network?" can often give you immediate confidence and jump-start your results. Walking into a room of 200 people uncertain of what you want to do, whom you want to meet, and what you want to say about yourself will only make you feel even more uncertain. On the other hand, walking into that same room knowing precisely which three people you would like to speak with gives you much more self-assuredness to go in there and do it. Even if you mingle with others in the meantime, being able to explicitly state your purpose for attending the event will make you feel more in control and more comfortable in that environment.

Try it sometime. Next time you go to a networking meeting and someone asks what brings you there, say, "You know, I really don't know." And see how you feel. Then contrast that with how you might feel if you said, "I'm hoping to meet some folks who do environmental litigation. It's a field I'm looking to break into."

Even if you love to network already and have all the confidence in the world, a strong, clear purpose is an indispensable guide. It'll keep you from being scattered with your efforts and direct you what to say *yes* to and what to say *no* to.

What is your main purpose for networking? *What do you want to do and by when?* Here are some examples:

- To find a director-level job in health-care marketing by May
- To double the number of coaching clients I have by the end of the year
- To get promoted in my company within the next 9 to 12 months
- To start my own interior design business by the fall
- To find five joint-venture partners within the next 6 months for my new-product launch

The more specific you get with your overall purpose, the easier it will be to pinpoint exactly whom you should be networking with and where to find them, which is the next step of your plan.

Write your purpose in Box 1 of your one-page plan (Figure 13.1). In the box above it, fill in the dates this specific plan will cover—today's date in the first space and the target end date in the second space. This doesn't mean you'll stop networking completely after the end date. It just gives you a target for completing the tasks on this specific plan. Afterwards, you might develop a new plan with an even higher goal and different tasks. Personally, I like planning periods of at least one quarter, but no longer than one year. You want to have enough time to complete enough activities on your plan to make significant progress toward your goal.

One last note: You may have several goals you are pursuing that involve networking. If they're closely related, it might make sense to roll them up into one overarching goal. If not, then create a separate plan for each. For example, if you want to advance within your company over the short term but, at the same time, start planning to launch your own business in the long term, there may be little overlap in actions and time frames so that each goal deserves its own plan.

2. Key Connections

Based on your goal, who are the people you need help from? Whom in your current network should you reconnect with? Who works in that industry? Who does what you want to do? Who's in a decision making role? Who are intermediaries that can introduce you to

Figure 13.1 Smart Networking One-Page Plan.

(You can download a free 8½-inch by 11-inch printable template of the one-page plan at www.smartnetworking.com.)

Smart Networking One-Page Plan

Planning Period: ___Jan 15___ to ___Jul 15___

1 Purpose: Why do I want to network? What's my goal?

Win 4 new marketing projects in the next six months

2 Key Connections: Whom do I need in my network to reach my goal?

	Who?	Why?	How?
1.	Kerry Collins	Catch up w/former client	Meet for lunch
2.	Jim Scott	Possible strategic alliance?	Meet for lunch
3.	Eleanor Steele	Potential speaking opp?	Local chapter meeting
4.	Marketing SVPs	Influencers to Chief Marketing	Industry conference
5.	Advertising Consultants	Possible referral partners?	Advertising Association
6.			
7.			
8.			
9.			
10.			

To maximize interactions, prepare a short list of questions to ask to learn more about others and uncover potential value you can provide.

3 Pitch: What's my standard pitch?

I help luxury brands expand their customer base and revenues

4 Key Activities: How should I focus my time?

One-Time

To set up right away:
- Redesign blog, add blogroll
- Outline case study for elevator pitch
-

To do at least once during the planning period:
- Speak at annual industry conference
-
-

Ongoing

Choose one 15--minute task to do each _day_ :
- Review Google alerts
- Write blog post
- Check friends' activities and comment
- Post marketing question on LinkedIn
- List questions to ask key connections
-
-

Choose one 1-hour task to do each _week_ :
- Comment on blogs
- Skim friends' pages for new connections
- Outline e-zine feature article
- Meet with key connection
-
-

Ad Hoc

To do as often as I can:
- Send referrals to my network
-
-

To do as needed:
- Respond to requests for help
- Attend board and committee meetings
-

decision makers? These are all people you should plan to connect with one-on-one.

Who else would be helpful in your networking, either individuals or groups, whom you have yet to meet? They will determine which connection strategies to use. If you want to work in health-care marketing but no one in your network works in either health care or marketing, it may make sense to join a local association in one or both of those industries to start meeting professionals already working in that field. Or, if you're interested in a specific company but no one you know works there, you might check your LinkedIn connections to see who's connected to someone who does.

The more specific you can be about who your target networking audience is, the more you can focus your efforts. If you're thinking everybody is your target, you'll find yourself running from meeting to meeting and event to event. Even worse, members of your network will give you referrals they think will help you, when in reality they'll just take up time. But you can't give specific direction to others if you're not clear in your own head about what you want.

When I first started networking, I spent a lot of time meeting with lots of people in different professions. Part of that was useful to help me figure out whom I really should be networking with. I eventually realized that for my strategy consulting company, there were more synergies with other consultants in marketing and business development fields, and not so much with technology consultants. We were less able to refer business to each other because we didn't talk to the same decision makers in a company.

Don't limit your thinking to just your end customers either. Think of influencers and possible referral partners you should connect with too. A mortgage broker could form alliances with real estate agents and real estate attorneys. A graphic designer could partner with a marketing communications consultant and a printer.

Who?

You have room to list up to 10 different contacts, either names of specific individuals (e.g., Sally Smith, a college classmate who worked in health care earlier in her career), or distinct groups of people you should meet (e.g., health-care professionals and marketing firms that work with health-care companies). You might have more than 10 different individuals and groups you could meet, but for now, narrow your scope to a top 10. This will keep you focused and give you some quick wins, while allowing you time for follow-up and other strengthening activities once you've made initial connections and reconnections.

Why?

In your plan, it's important to articulate why it makes sense to connect with each person or group. As the purpose statement in Box 1 will guide your overall networking efforts, listing a specific purpose for connecting with each person or group will guide your interactions with them. Some you'll meet for the purpose of gathering information about industry trends, while others are potential alliance partners. When you set up your meetings, you'll be able to relay a specific purpose for getting together and have a focused conversation, which will impress your contacts, make them receptive to networking with you, and help them determine how best they can help you.

How?

The people you want to meet will guide which connection strategies you use. In this space, write down how you intend to connect with each individual or group on your list. For someone you already know, a face-to-face meeting might be the best option. For a group of people, going to an event that attracts that crowd or joining an online community that focuses on that industry might be a good way to meet a lot of them at one time. Then figure out later whom to build deeper relationships with.

Don't be afraid to get creative about how to connect with the people you really want to meet. When a good friend was having difficulty arranging her crucial business school interview with an alumnus who was always traveling, she found out he was going to be attending a wedding at Disney World in Florida one weekend. After checking out prices for flights, she let him know that "by coincidence" she would be in the area as well. "We agreed to meet up in the Polynesian Village, had the interview over a Hawaiian drink, and then went our separate ways for some Disney entertainment. I got into the business school, and the rest is history!"

3. Pitch

There will be elements of your pitch already included in your overall purpose, but it's an important enough element of networking that it should be a distinct part of your one-page plan. And since you're going to be saying it all throughout your networking lifespan, I wanted to give it its own space. If you need to, review Chapter 4 on developing your pitch, and write out at least your first-level pitch in Box 3 so you can readily describe what you do in one focused sentence.

4. Key Activities

This section is the core of your plan—your networking to-do list. Once you've figured out whom you need to build relationships with, why they're important to you, and how you might reach out to them, then your networking actions should revolve around getting yourself known, liked, and trusted by them. Based on your goals, timeline, and preferences, you'll be better able to choose the right blend of in-person and online networking tools to use to make that happen.

The key activities section is set up to give you enough flexibility to determine your own tasks and timing, while also providing enough structure to make sure you're covering all the bases:

- *One-time activities* that are either an up-front setup task or a longer-term tactic that you'll pursue at least once
- *Ongoing activities* that you'll do on a regular basis, separated into quick 15-minute tasks and those that can take an hour or more
- *Ad hoc activities* that you can do as often as you like or as often as you need to

With a quick glance at your plan, you can see what needs to be done and what you might have time to do. If you know you're facing a really busy week, you can still find time for one 15-minute task to do early one morning before you start work. On the other hand, if your schedule is a bit more open, you might tackle one or more of the 1-hour tasks.

Everyone's list will be different. Even if you and I have the same overall goal and a similar list of actions, we may put them in different sections based on our timeline and preferences. For instance, I love to write and would probably put more writing tasks—blog entries, e-zine articles—in the *ongoing* section and put in-person

meetings in the *as needed* column. You might have completely oppo-
site preferences.

One-Time Activities

These are tasks that you must do up front to make the rest of your plan
work, or tasks that you'd like to try doing at least once.

Examples of *key setup tasks* might include:

- Create online profiles on LinkedIn and Facebook.
- Convert current contact list into an opt-in e-mail list.
- Set up my blog.
- Research industry associations, networking groups, and
  conferences that might attract my key connections.
- Brainstorm examples and stories for my elevator pitch.

Examples of *at-least-once tasks* include:

- Give a presentation to my department.
- Have lunch with my division president.
- Attend or speak at an industry conference.
- Write an article for a trade association newsletter.

If you prefer, you can plan to do these *at-least-once tasks* more frequently by putting them in the *as often as I can* section. It's completely
your decision.

Ongoing Activities

These are typically maintenance tasks that you should do on a consistent basis to keep in touch with members of your network and stay on
their radar screens. They're divided up into two columns to distinguish
quick 15-minute tasks from longer 1-hour tasks.

Examples of *15-minute tasks* might include:

- Set up a meeting with one of my key connections.
- Write a blog post.
- Skim friends' profiles for new friends and connections to add.
- Browse LinkedIn Answers for interesting questions.
- Skim a favorite blog.
- Check news feeds and Google Alerts.

Examples of *1-hour tasks* might include:

* Have a face-to-face meeting with a key connection.
* Review one new social networking tool.
* Add content to online profiles.
* Publish e-zine.

You decide how frequently you want to perform each column of activities. Do you want to do something small every day, or is once a week all you can manage? How often can you set aside one hour or more for a networking task? If you have an aggressive goal, you might carve out this hour in your schedule once a week. If your goal is longer term, completing one big activity a month or quarter might be just fine. It's totally up to you. Just pick one time period—day, week, month, or quarter—for each column.

Here are some initial guidelines to think about, but your plan is totally flexible and you can decide what works best for you:

* *An entrepreneur or salesperson* who is constantly networking and marketing for new clients might choose one 15-minute task per *day* and one 1-hour task per *week*.
* *An active but employed job seeker* might choose one 15-minute task per *week* and one 1-hour task per *month*.
* *A career advancer* might have an even longer planning period and decide on one 15-minute task per *month* and one 1-hour task per *quarter*.

Ad Hoc Activities
These are tasks that you want to keep on your list as reminders but that you won't do with predetermined frequency.

Examples of *as-often-as-I-can tasks* might include:

* Send referrals to my network.
* Comment on industry-leading blogs.
* Attend a local association event.
* Forward helpful articles or info.

Examples of *as-needed tasks* might include:

- Write a thank you note or e-mail.
- Send follow-up e-mails after an event.

Final Words on Using Your Plan

I started you off with a few ideas for each section of your plan, but of course there are many more tasks you can add. Get creative, use your imagination, and most of all, do as much of what you like to do while understanding that you may have to include a few tasks that aren't your favorites but are necessary in order to reach your goals more quickly.

Feel free to put any of the task examples into any area of the key activities section you choose, depending on how often you want to do them. You should have a couple of tasks listed in every section so you're always balancing immediate versus long term and discrete versus ongoing.

Keep your plan by your desk so you can refer to it easily. Ideally, find a buddy or two to work with to develop your plans and hold each other accountable. You can brainstorm ideas about key connections and activities, give feedback on your pitches, and set deadlines and rewards. You can even create a small work group at your office or in your department to come up with a plan for networking and collaborating more effectively throughout your company and identify the actions each person will take. With this kind of support, you'll be reaching your goals in no time.

CLOSING THOUGHTS

FINAL LESSONS AND ONE LAST CHALLENGE

Five years from now you will be pretty much the same as you are today except for two things: the books you read and the people you get close to.

—*Charles Jones*

If a book has the ability to change the reader, then it certainly should have as profound an effect on the writer. Right?

What surprised me more than being changed through writing, however, is *how* it changed me. While I expected that researching the topic and articulating these concepts would expand and clarify my thoughts and feelings about networking, it's really the people I've met (mostly virtually) and the stories they've told me (more than I had room for on these pages) that have reinforced my beliefs even more. Here are the lessons I learned from them that can give you a push if you ever feel stuck.

If You're Not Inspired by the People around You, Go Meet Some New People

For those who have complained to me in the past that they just can't get interested in the people they meet while networking, this is my new recommendation. If you fall into this camp, perhaps the problem isn't with networking per se, but that you simply have not yet found your tribe. I'm no extrovert, as I've said multiple times, but over the last few months, I've met more people I'd like to get to know better than I have slots in my calendar for the next year. My list of Facebook friends tripled just from the time I started writing to when I finished the first draft just a few months later, many of them doing cool things I'd like to learn more about and get involved with. Interesting people are out there, and now there are relatively easy ways to find them if you really want to.

The Worst Thing about Networking Is the Word Itself, but That Shouldn't Stop You

"Networking" is a term in desperate need of a brand image change. "Social networking" is less cringe-inducing, but only because there's a tech aspect to it so it seems cooler. The basic relationship-building tenets still apply. When I worked on the proposal for this book, I really wanted to come up with a different word for networking, but all the variations sounded forced or contrived. What I found in writing this book is that few who experience success with networking really think about the word that much. What they're focused on is finding people of like minds and interests, exchanging ideas, and seeing whether the sum can be greater than the parts. What it's called is almost irrelevant. Perhaps Madison Avenue will eventually coin a new phrase, but don't stop short of your dreams waiting for that to happen. It's just a word after all.

If You Can't Find a Networking Activity to Suit Your Needs, You're Not Looking Hard Enough

There isn't one right way to network, and no one personality type is needed to succeed with it. All the people mentioned in this book are different. Some are power networkers; most aren't. Some feel more comfortable face-to-face, others prefer to focus online. Some blog, others Tweet, some do both and more. I've made plenty of suggestions for networking effectively, and you can find more at www.smartnetworking. com. There's no shortage of ideas for building and maintaining relationships to help you reach your goals, and each of them works for *someone*. Don't dismiss one before you've given it a fair shot.

We'll All Be Better If We Help Others Be Better

In reading through all the stories I received and seeing the successes achieved, I can't help but think how much we and the people around us could accomplish if everyone realized the importance of networking and invested the time in learning how to do it effectively. Imagine if our employees learned how to build strong relationships both inside and outside the company. Teamwork and collaboration would be elevated from mere buzzwords to real practice, and the resulting ROI would be off the charts. Or what if our college students knew how to leverage the hundreds or thousands of contacts they make during their years on campus? Could they literally recession-proof their careers? I really think so.

My closing challenge to you, then, is this: Jack Canfield said in *The Success Principles*, "When you lift up others, they will lift you up." I encourage you to help the people who matter most to you—your family, your friends, your customers, your students, your staff—develop these critical relationship-building skills by sharing the concepts in this book with them. Inspire other readers of this book by posting your own networking success stories on our Web site. Assist others more broadly by being a role model for them with your own networking best practices. There's a lot of good you can do and a lot of good people around you to do it for.

I wish you great success in your networking journey and may our paths cross often in person, online, or both.

BIBLIOGRAPHY

Alba, Jason, *I'm on LinkedIn—Now What???: A Guide to Getting the Most OUT of LinkedIn* (Cupertino, CA: Happy About, 2007).

Alba, Jason, and Jesse Stay, *I'm on Facebook—Now What???: How to Get Personal, Business, and Professional Value from Facebook* (Cupertino, CA: Happy About, 2008).

Anderson, Chris, *The Long Tail: Why the Future of Business Is Selling Less of More* (New York: Hyperion, 2006).

Burg, Bob, *Endless Referrals: Network Your Everyday Contacts into Sales*, new and updated ed. (New York: McGraw-Hill, 2005).

Canfield, Jack, *The Success Principles: How to Get from Where You Are to Where You Want to Be* (New York: HarperCollins, 2005).

Carnegie, Dale, *How to Win Friends and Influence People*, reprint ed. (New York: Pocket Books, 1998).

Cook, John, *The Book of Positive Quotations* (Minneapolis: Fairview Press, 1993).

Covey, Stephen M. R., *The Speed of Trust: The One Thing That Changes Everything* (New York: The Free Press, 2008).

Covey, Stephen R., *The 7 Habits of Highly Effective People: Powerful Lessons in Personal Change* (New York: The Free Press, 2004).

Curtis, Bryan, *Classic Wisdom for the Good Life* (Nashville: Rutledge Hill Press, 2006).

Ferriss, Timothy, *The 4-Hour Workweek: Escape 9–5, Live Anywhere, and Join the New Rich* (New York: Crown Publishing, 2007).

Gladwell, Malcolm, *The Tipping Point: How Little Things Can Make a Big Difference* (New York: Back Bay Books, 2002).

Godin, Seth, *Permission Marketing: Turning Strangers into Friends and Friends into Customers* (New York: Simon & Schuster, 1999).

Hill, Napoleon, *Think and Grow Rich* (North Hollywood, CA: Wilshire Book Company, 1999).

Laney, Marti Olsen, *The Introvert Advantage: How to Thrive in an Extrovert World* (New York: Workman Publishing Company, 2002).

Leeds, Dorothy, *The 7 Powers of Questions: Secrets to Successful Communication in Life and at Work* (New York: Perigee Trade, 2000).

Mandese, Joe, "Hitting the Wall," *MediaPost Publications*, February 24, 2008.

Nierenberg, Andrea R., *Million Dollar Networking: The Sure Way to Find, Keep and Grow Your Business* (Sterling, VA: Capital Books, 2005).

Pulver, Jeff, "Confessions of a LinkedIn Dropout," *BusinessWeek*, August 6, 2007.

Sanders, Tim, *The Likeability Factor: How to Boost Your L-Factor and Achieve Your Life's Dreams* (New York: Three Rivers Press, 2006).

Scoble, Robert, and Shel Israel, *Naked Conversations: How Blogs Are Changing the Way Businesses Talk with Customers* (Hoboken, NJ: John Wiley & Sons, 2006).

Tracy, Brian, and Ron Arden, *The Power of Charm: How to Win Anyone Over in Any Situation* (New York: AMACOM, 2006).

INDEX

ABOUT THE AUTHOR

Liz Lynch, founder of the Center for Networking Excellence, is passionate about helping business professionals network smart by teaching them to strive for 24/7 results without 24/7 effort. Her bottom-line approach grew from her experience in corporate America working at some of the top firms in their industries. Before pursuing an entrepreneurial path, Liz honed her strategic, analytical, and financial expertise at Goldman Sachs, Disney, Booz & Company, and Time Warner. She also holds an engineering degree from the University of California, Berkeley and an MBA from Stanford University.

Because of her background, Liz brings a practical and insightful perspective to networking that has connected with a global audience. She has been invited to speak at organizations and conferences around the world, her popular *102 Secrets to Smarter Networking* booklet and related audio programs have sold on six continents, and her writings have been translated into multiple languages.

Born in the Philippines and raised in the San Francisco Bay Area, Liz now lives with her husband in New York City.

For information on products, programs, and speaking availability, visit www.NetworkingExcellence.com.